THE STREETS OF WEST HAMPSTEAD

West End, 1840, by H. Fancourt, with West End Hall (centre) and the Cock & Hoop (right).

THE STREETS OF WEST HAMPSTEAD

A survey of streets, houses and residents
in the western sector of
the old borough of Hampstead

Compiled by
**CAMDEN HISTORY SOCIETY'S
STREET HISTORY GROUP**

and edited by
CHRISTOPHER WADE

CAMDEN HISTORY SOCIETY
1992

First edition of this survey published by the High Hill Press in 1975. *Completely revised and enlarged 1992*

© **Camden History Society 1992**

ISBN 0–904491–34–X

Typeset and design by Historical Publications Ltd. Printed by Printpoint Ltd, Broadfield Lane, NW1.

Most pictures have come from Camden's Local Studies Library. Our thanks to them and also to the following for providing illustrations:
Hampstead Museum, Historical Publications, Dr. W. Levy, National Portrait Gallery, Pelican Books, Powell-Cotton family, Jean Smith, Allan Wingate.

CONTENTS

MAIN SOURCES

Books

Boyd Alexander: *England's Wealthiest Son* (Centaur Press, 1962)

F.E. Baines: *Records of the Manor of Hampstead* (Whitaker, 1890)

T.F.T. Baker (ed): *The Victoria County History of Middlesex* Vol IX (OUP, 1989)

Adeline Barnes: *Reminiscences of West End* (MS 1883, at Swiss Cottage Library)

Thomas J. Barratt: *Annals of Hampstead* (Black, 1912; Lionel Leventhal Ltd, 1972)

Gillian Bebbington: *London Street Names* (Batsford, 1987)

Charles Booth: *Life and Labour of the People in London* (Macmillan, 1892–7)

Basil Clarke: *Parish Churches of London* (Batsford, 1966)

Michael Collins (ed): Catalogue of *Hampstead in the Thirties* (an exhibition arranged by Hampstead Artists' Council, 1974)

A.M. Eyre: *History of St John's Wood* (Chapman & Hall, 1913)

Ford Madox Ford: *Songs from London* (Elkin Mathews, 1910)

Florence Hardy: *The Life of Thomas Hardy* (Macmillan, 1933)

Trevor Jennings: *The School in Mill Lane* (1973)

F.R.D'O Monro: *A History of Hampstead Cricket Club* (Home and Van Thal, 1949)

J.J. Park: *The Topography and Natural History of Hampstead* (Nichols, Son & Bentley, 1814/18)

Reginald Pound & Geoffrey Harmsworth: *Northcliffe* (Cassell, 1959)

John Richardson: *Hampstead One Thousand* (Historical Publications, 1985)

F.M.L. Thompson: *Hampstead – Building a Borough 1650–1964* (Routledge & Kegan Paul, 1974)

Alec Waugh: *The Early Years* (Cassell, 1962)

Evelyn Waugh: *A Little Learning* (Chapman & Hall, 1964)

Maps

1746	Rocque
1814	Park/Newton
1829/35	Cruchley
1830	Greenwood
1839	Tithe Map
1862	Weller
1862	Stanford
1864	Daw
1866/71	Ordnance Survey
1883/91	Lowe
1889/98	Booth's Poverty Maps

Other Sources

Camden Local Studies Library at Swiss Cottage Library: Manor Minute Books, Street Directories, Census Returns, Rate Books

The Hampstead and Highgate Express

The Kilburn Times

LCC Street Lists

The Greater London Record Office

R.I.B.A. Library

Department of the Environment's List of Buildings of Historic or Architectural Interest

Camden History Reviews

The Dictionary of National Biography (OUP) abbreviated as *DNB*

INTRODUCTION

'West Hampstead need be visited only by those in search of Victorian churches,' declared Nikolaus Pevsner in his *Buildings of England* series.'The houses and streets require no notice.'

This was a splendid challenge to our local history society, which decided in the 1970s to survey all the streets of the old borough of Hampstead, and eventually published the findings in three volumes. *The Streets of Hampstead* (revised 1984) was followed by *More Streets of Hampstead* (revised as *The Streets of Belsize*, 1991) and by *The Streets of West Hampstead* in 1975. In this last volume, the first ever book about West Hampstead, we quoted Professor Pevsner's verdict – and we invited him to the book launch. He sportingly came and delightfully 'declared the book open'.

West Hampstead begins at Finchley Road and ends halfway across Kilburn High Road, which is the border with Brent. 'It is not a well-known part of London,' said a learned article in the *Journal of the Anthropological Society of Oxford* (1988). 'It has no particular attraction for tourists or visitors, though it has many advantages as a residential area.'

As we said in our first edition, the pleasures of West Hampstead streets are found with some difficulty and in the most unlikely places. They are, therefore, all the more rewarding to discover. Apart from a score of DOE Listed Buildings, some included for 'curiosity value', there are rows of decorated terraces showing the exuberance of the Victorian builder. You can find sunflowers in Sumatra Road, ferns in Mazenod, dragons in Inglewood and Woodchurch. As for the street names, they range romantically from Gascony to Parsifal, from Agamemnon to Narcissus and, surprisingly, from Skardu to Weech.

There is no shortage of remarkable residents. Here are Thomas Hardy in Kilburn High Road, Lillie Langtry in Alexandra Road, Alec and Evelyn Waugh in Hillfield Road, A.A. Milne and H.G. Wells in Mortimer Crescent. T.S. Eliot and George Orwell put in brief appearances. Artists include Bomberg, Coldstream and Sickert. William Beckford, Fanny Brawne and Leigh Hunt all lived here. Among more recent residents we meet Sir Adrian Boult, Sir Dirk Bogarde, Jim Laker and Kim Philby. Only Lord Northcliffe and William Friese-Greene have achieved blue plaques. Current residents of note include two writers: Doris Lessing and John Hillaby; two Royal Academicians: Norman Blamey and Willi Soukop; and two chess Grand Masters: Nigel Short and Jonathan Speelman.

Then there is the lively social history of an area fragmented suddenly by four different railway systems in the mid-nineteenth century. As the stations opened, the Stately Homes of the village of West End closed down. Landowners cashed in on the chaos and caused the rapid growth of a densely-packed, socially-mixed district. Men of religion were rightly worried. 'The people came before the churches and so acquired habits of neglect', according to Charles Booth. Towards the end of the century, this 'strange and difficult district' caused further concern when it acquired so many blocks of flats: it was generally thought that people living in flats were ignoring their domestic responsibilities.

In the twentieth century, West Hampstead life has been affected by the influx of Jewish refugees in the Thirties, by the bombing (especially near the railways) in the last war, and by the widening of Finchley Road in the 1960s, creating a great divide between upper and lower Hampstead. Since the war, large sections of West Hampstead have been turned into council estates, some innovative and imaginative in design. But as local redevelopment policy softened in the 1970s, many of the buildings noted in our original survey as being ripened for demolition were spared and even refurbished. With this trend came the gentrification of some streets (as recognised in an article in *New Society* in 1982) and, more recently, the creation of Conservation Areas. Inevitably, most of the small family houses to the west of West End Lane have been split up into flats and single rooms, but the Lane has kept its small shops and the community spirit has survived.

The members of our Street History Group for this book and the main areas that they researched were: John Davies (Eyre Estate), Christina Gee (Abbey Farm and Powell-Cottons Again), Yvonne Melnick (Powell-Cotton Estate and Mill Lane), Susan Palmer (Iverson Road, Kilburn High Road and Finchley Road), Charles Regan (East of West End Lane), Dilys Thomas (Maryon Wilson), Margaret and Richard Vaughan (Fortune Green), Christopher Wade (*passim*) and Dick Weindling (West End). The last named has researched West Hampstead truly, widely and deeply, and was able to help in many areas.

The original surveyors whose researches and writings created the first edition were Shirley Harris, Jenepher Hawkins, Anthony Moss and Wilfrid Meadows. Much credit to them and to Ian Norrie of High Hill Press, our first publisher.

Apart from pounding the pavements of West Hampstead, we found most of our facts at Camden's Local Studies Library at Swiss Cottage, where the Librarian, Malcolm Holmes, and his colleagues, especially Valerie Hart and Lesley Marshall, were ever helpful. The recently published *Victoria County History* volume covering Hampstead was of great assistance: our other printed sources are listed at the front.

Thanks for additional information go to Jean Smith, Wendy Trewin, Caroline Woollett, Michael Alpert, Margaret Holmes, Roger Rowley and members of the Powell-Cotton family; for word-processing and indexing to Susan Palmer and for photography to Geoffrey Kaye. As ever, we readily acknowledge that our survey cannot be infallible or exhaustive and we invite our readers to point out any serious errors or omissions in their usual understanding way.

Christopher Wade
Hampstead, December 1991.

AROUND THE GREEN

A report of the Great Plague of London in 1665 noted that 'At Hampstead died two hundred, three score and odd...yet at West End, a little village a quarter of a mile off, at the bottom of the hill, there died none, though there are about 30 or 40 houses there'.

Separated as it now is from the heights of Hampstead by the traffic barrier of Finchley Road, West End seems more remote from the main part of Hampstead than it did in the days when only fields intervened. Although, in fact, nearer as the crow flies to the Parish Church than are either South End or North End, it was nevertheless more secluded in feeling than either of these other two and also more attractive because of its position by the stream on some of the better farming land of the parish.

In medieval times the hamlet of West End was held of the Abbot of Westminster by the Prioress of Kilburn. In the reign of Henry VIII its estimated area was eighteen acres and by the middle of the eighteenth century it contained, according to Park, upwards of forty houses. The road junction at West End Green was the obvious place for growth to occur and, until comparatively modern development overtook the area, there were no houses between West End itself and Kilburn.

Growth was slow. The 1804 Directory listed eight house-holders of independent means. In the 1841 Census there were still only eight such householders though the names were different. Between 1841 and 1871, the population rose from about 370 only to about 570 people. They inhabited the pleasant, sometimes large, houses which lined the Green as far south as West End House (see plan). Some of these houses dated to the 17th century, which indicates that West End must even then have been judged an attractive retreat. It may be that it grew up from a farming settlement into a hamlet simply through the influence of these houses. Certainly, until the arrival of Thomas Potter's foundry (see below) and the various railways, the population was small and disinclined to welcome strangers. It was so peaceful that the striking of Big Ben could be heard and, indeed, the owners of West End Hall were sure that in 1815 they had heard the sounds of the cannon at Waterloo. Amenities were few. The Cock and Hoop tavern and the baker supplied basic wants, while a few other items such as coal and potatoes could be bought at the beerhouses opposite West End Hall. Despite its rural remoteness, however, from the time of London's growth westwards to Hyde Park, West End Lane must have provided a convenient route to Hampstead from Mayfair and thereabouts. It was obviously much simpler to drive up the Edgware Road and

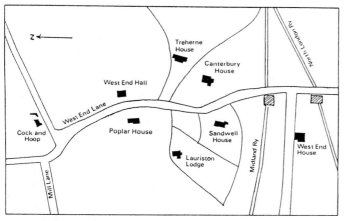

1. *Plan of West End in the 1860s*, showing the main buildings.

2. *West End Hall* (later called West End House), *c*1890, from a watercolour by Harold Lawes.

turn off at Kilburn than to take the more frequented route through Camden Town, and, as Queen Victoria herself enjoyed the drive, it would be likely that other and earlier residents of her part of London would have done the same.

At the beginning of the nineteenth century, probably the only very large houses were West End House, West End Hall and Lauriston Lodge. At this time, the Beckford family owned West End House, the southernmost of them all. Also residing in West End were the magistrate, Germain Lavie, leading light in the suppression of West End Fair and one of four gentlemen who in 1807 bought up a section of the Belsize Estate; another magistrate, Josiah Boydell (see Inglewood Road), and, in his own time a lesser figure though to us the best known, Leigh Hunt, who lived in a cottage there in 1812 on a site near the present Fire Station.'A real bona fide cottage' he wrote to a friend, 'with humble ceilings and unsophisticated staircase: but there is a green about it, and a garden with laurels'. But the poet did not stay here long as he was convicted of libelling the Prince Regent in his newspaper *The Examiner* and jailed for two years. (For his later residence in the Vale of Health, see *The Streets of Hampstead*.) During the century the larger houses continued to proliferate around the Green until the arrival of the railways in the 1860s destroyed the peace and seclusion: slowly the gentry left and the field lay open to the developers.

The families of West End tended to change fairly frequently as the houses were customarily let furnished. There was, however, one exception to this: the Miles family of West End Hall both lived in the house they owned and remained there for the greater part of the century. They became the nearest approach to a local 'squire' that West End had. Mr and Mrs John Miles first went to live in the house upon their marriage in 1813. They brought up their family there and the connection did not end until Mrs Miles, by then a widow of 98, died there in 1889. The family was renowned locally for its philanthropic works and played a large part in the foundation of the West End National School (see Emmanuel School).

The Fair, which was held annually on **West End Green** until 1821, lasted for three days, from 26–28 July. Its origins had been quite informal, a little local festivity consisting of, to quote Germain Lavie, 'four or five Toy and Gingerbread Booths only and a single Show'. From the owners of these booths the Lord of the Manor received a rent, the Green being manorial waste. A local cowkeeper allowed the fair to overflow into the field which he rented and, as the boundaries of London were coming ever nearer, the event began to attract gangs of hooligans and thieves. Attempts by the local gentry to suppress it began in 1812, but it was not until nine years later that it finally disappeared. A newspaper account of 1819 shows what dangers it had begun to hold for ordinary, peaceable patrons. It tells of a man knocked down by a gang of over sixty men and boys. His clothes were almost torn from him and he escaped only because he was thrown through the canvas of a music booth, where some of the fiddlers helped him to repel the gang. In this year also, a clergyman stated that a crowd of two hundred 'London roughs' gathered there and cut the clothes from people's backs, so that the special constables had to be called in to suppress the disorder. Of the many arrested, four were sentenced to death and others deported to Botany Bay. Another small, but happier, source of fame for West End Green is that it was reputed to have been the site of the last maypole near London.

The pond which was once to be found on the Green was part of the stream which came down through a brick drain from Branch Hill, followed the line of Cannon Hill and West End Lane as far as about Dennington Park Road and then flowed away down the hill to join the Kilburn. The stream, which is now underground, flowed under the foot of Kilburn High Road (an area still known as Kilburn Bridge) and joined the River Westbourne which filled the Serpentine before reaching the Thames near Chelsea Bridge. In hot weather the pond on the Green would dry up and become a source of infection, and it was through the efforts of the indefatigable Dr Lord, Hampstead's first Medical Officer of Health, that it was filled in. Piped water was laid on to most houses by the 1860s.

West End nearly lost its Green in 1875; it was 'granted' to John Culverhouse by the Lord of the Manor who had, within certain limits, the right to dispose of manorial waste in this way. Mr Culverhouse, intending to sell the land for building, had a hoarding set up around it, but this was pulled down by the local people. So the situation remained until the summer of 1882 when a Mr Fowle, who had arranged to buy the land for £850, set up a much stronger hoarding and began to strip off the turf. A protest meeting was held at Emmanuel School and, one wet Monday night soon after, some two hundred locals converged to demolish the boards and burn them on the Green. Eight men were arrested but were found 'not guilty' by the magistrates. At the trial, evidence was given that the Green had been a recreation ground 'from time immemorial'. Three years later the Vestry bought the Green for the same price of £850.

DOWN THE LANE

The stretch of **WEST END LANE** which leads down from Finchley Road to the Green is relatively short and shows why so many of the residents of West End were opposed to the new road to Finchley in the 1820s. It would have been seen as a means of bringing possibly undesirable strangers too unhealthily close to home.

The hill descends between the heights of **Buckingham** and **Cumberland Mansions**, which have similar sunflower balconies. At the foot of the hill on the south side used to be two small houses, Fern Cottage and Lawn Cottage. The occupant of the latter house in the 1870s was the successful miniaturist, Robert Henderson (1826–1904), whose family were well known in the Vale of Health for over a century. Across the road, on the site of **Alexandra Mansions**, was The Cock and Hoop, for many years the only tavern in West End. Established by 1720 and always deeply involved in the life of the community, The Cock and Hoop was closed in 1896 after a number of minor irregularities. The main problem had been that when the police came to deliver a summons for watering the whisky, they found that the licensee named over the front door had been dead for four years. Added to this, there was opposition from local temperance campaigners and from the newly built Emmanuel Church. (The full story is told in *Camden History Re-*view No. 9.) Alexandra Mansions were built in 1902 (date over door) and named after the new Queen, incidentally the patron of the Hearts of Oak Benefit Society, which loaned £10,000 for the development. The coronation of Edward VII in the same year is commemorated by an **oak tree** (with plaque) on the Green. The granite **fountain** nearby was erected in 1897 by a daughter of the Miles family in memory of her mother.

The south-west corner of the Green, where the Lane turns left, has seen a great succession of changes. Before the row of shops **Nos. 327–341**, there were two houses, The Elms and The Cedars, built in 1880 by Thomas Potter junior. The Cedars was named after the trees in the garden of an even older house on this site called West End Lodge, with a moat at the back of the property. The Elms became the first parsonage of Emmanuel Church in 1882 and, soon after, the home of Sir William Onslow, an ex-High Sheriff of Cornwall. The houses were replaced by **Cavendish Parade** in 1903 (see date). The **Fire Station** is certainly the most attractive building now standing in this area, and the only one to be a Listed building. According to the List it dates from 1901 and was designed 'by W.A. Scott...in Voysey manner'. Previously a horse-drawn voluntary brigade operated from the bottom of Kilburn High Road. At the rear of the Station, a terrace of **firemen's cottages** of the same date and architect is also Listed. On the site of **Cavendish Motors** and **Carlton House** were until 1930 three eighteenth-century houses known as Nos. 1, 2 and 3 The Green. Two artists of repute lived at No. 2 – Charles Bestland (1763–c1837), another miniaturist and engraver, and Alfred Slocombe, a painter and etcher (see Iverson Road).

Down a private lane to the west, **Salmon's Garages** and **Flats** are a group of late Victorian stables, probably built for the adjoining **Welbeck Mansions** (see Inglewood Road). These mansion flats occupy the site of the small brass and iron foundry built by Thomas Potter senior in 1861 and demolished in 1897. Apart from the railways, this was the first non-residential development in the area. From this foundry came much of the metalwork for the outer screen walls of the Law Courts in the Strand. This was one of several occasions when Potter worked with the distinguished architect, G.E. Street. His foundry also specialised in brass lecterns and one of these has been identified in St Barnabas, Pimlico. The Potters' showroom was at 44 South Molton Street from 1846 to 1906 and later in Victoria Street. As Mr Potter found it difficult to house his workers, he built **West Cottages**. In 1862 six were built and five years later there were seven more: on the 1866 OS map they were called Potter's Buildings. With their original attractive facades, especially on **Nos. 8–13**, these cottages are among the few relics of old West End still remaining. According to *Reminiscences of West End* by Mrs Adeline Barnes, the enterprising Mr Potter tried to make his own gas and built a gasometer for this purpose, but opposition made him give up the idea and it was used as a water tank until the foundry closed down. To support this last point, the 1873 Directory shows No. 1 West End Cottages occupied by two turn-

cocks of the West Middlesex Waterworks.

Next along the road, between **Inglewood Mansions** and the pub, was a group of cottages called Providence Place, reputedly built in the seventeenth century as part of a farmhouse. The **Old Black Lion**, rebuilt in 1912, was established by 1751 as a beerhouse rather than as a tavern. It has outstayed its nearby rival, The Black Horse, which fell out of the running in the 1860s. Next door may be seen the upper storeys of two of the original cottages in this row, **Nos. 291–3**. As is usual with main road development of this kind, the shop fronts have taken in what used to be the front garden of the cottages and so the building has moved forward. Further down, a new pub called **Arkwright's Wheel** has been built and furnished in a totally Victorian

3. *The Old Black Lion*, West End Lane: a turn-of-the-century photograph.

style. In the 1890s, **Nos. 273–9** were called Dennington Parade and No. 273 opened then as Twigg and Foat, Iron-mongers. Sydney Venning took this business over in 1918 and his popular hardware store has only recently closed. Above **No. 255** may still be seen a sign Dennington Promenarde [*sic*], a name which also dates back to the 1890s. **No. 243** began then as a chemist's, and from 1904 to 1989 was known as Alban Atkin. In 1899, the whole road officially became West End Lane, after some claims by map-makers and West Enders that it might be called Kilburn Lane.

On the other side of the road near the Green was once the local bakery, which became also the Post Office. The rest of the Lane as far as Fawley Road, roughly **Nos. 208–268**, consisted of the frontage of West End Hall, the home of the Miles family. This house, sometimes known as New West End House to distinguish it from the original West End House further south, became, after the latter disappeared in 1870, the most substantial property, and, according to Baines in 1890, the oldest house in the area. He wrote that it was a 'roomy redbrick mansion, built probably at the end of the seventeenth century'. Between about 1798 and 1807 it was evidently occupied by the family of the Hon. Horatio Walpole, though Barratt has put them in the older West End House. John Miles, a book publisher, took the house in 1813. His wife was a local Lady Bountiful and welfare worker, who organised savings clubs for coal, clothing and blankets for the poor of the parish. During the Miles' time a watchman was employed to walk round the boundaries of the property and, according to Mrs Barnes, he would call the time on the hour. She also told of the

reputed ghost of a headless lady dressed in rustling silk skirts, who used to walk along the carriage drive to the gates. The elderly Mrs Miles held large haymaking parties in the grounds up to the year before her death in 1889.

The front of the West End Hall estate was built up at the turn of the century, leaving a space, represented by the white block of **Queen's Mansions**, where the entrance gates were. Until that time there was along the frontage a cobbled footpath and a row of twenty elms with a low wall behind them. In 1890, General Sir Charles Fraser, V.C., the new owner, wished to straighten out his front wall, which had an inward curve. The Vestry agreed, but after a public meeting which met to object that this action would mean the General's acquiring a considerable part of the footpath (ten yards in width at the widest point) and nine of the elm trees, the Vestry was obliged to cancel its permission. The General, however, claimed the cobblestones from the path. This last owner of West End Hall never lived at the house but kept it for three large garden parties he held in the season. Bus loads of staff would arrive one day, followed by the band of his regiment (the 7th Hussars) and eventually guests in their carriages. It was after the General died in 1897 that the final sale of the estate took place and the house was demolished. The spacious grounds, containing a lake and thirteen acres of woodland, might have become a public park. A subscription list was set up to raise £42,000, but in vain. The estate was sold for building development and West Hampstead lost its opportunity to acquire a green, ready-made open space.

Next to West End Hall, near the present **Bennet Court**, was the entrance to another large mansion, Treherne House. This stood in a triangle-shaped piece of ground with virtually no frontage at all except for the gates, and

4. *Sidney Venning's shop at 273 West End Lane.*

was thus in an extremely secluded position. It was a long, two-storey house (Thompson has a picture of it) built in 1815 by Thomas Bean. The most notable occupants were the famous sculptors, Robert Shout and his son Charles, whose family lived here from 1831–55. Robert was Master of the London Masons in 1822 and the family was immortalised by Shelley's line about Leigh Hunt's studio '…no doubt, Is still adorned with many a cast by Shout'. The house was considerably enlarged by its final owner, Sir John Fletcher, a wealthy solicitor, who became MP for Hampstead 1905–18 and a deputy chairman of the London County Council. He lived here from 1865 to 1897, when the property was redeveloped into the Fawley Road area. At the corner of Lymington Road **Canterbury Mansions** shows the approximate location of Canterbury House which, together with Sandwell House on the other side of West End Lane, was erected in 1862. Both big white houses were built in the Italian style by the Greenwood Brothers, contractors working on the Midland Railway. In his book *Suffolk Punch*, George Cross remembers Canterbury House and its last occupant, Anthony Lister, whose firm was the largest manufacturer of straw hats in England. From his father's butcher's shop on the site of the West Hampstead Library (see Dennington Park Road), young George would watch Lister drive off to the office in his imposing carriage with its 'old red-apple-faced, grey-whiskered coachman and the upright young footman, in their light-fawn uniforms and cockaded top hats'.

Behind Sandwell House was Lauriston Lodge (see Kingdon Road) and to the south, approximately between the present **Nos. 187–235**, stretched the wall of the West End House estate. Not only has the house gone but the twenty-one acre estate has been so cut up by the various railways which converge on this point that even the contours of the land have changed. The mansion stood facing the hamlet on a spot about two hundred yards along the south side of Iverson Road, and the carriage drive, instead of seeking the shortest route to the roadway, emphasised the house's connection with West End by heading north; it met the Lane with an imposing entrance gate and two lodges at what is now the eastern end of Sandwell Crescent. From 1775 this was the stately home of the Beckford family. William Beckford, whose fortune came from Jamaican sugar plantations, was twice Lord Mayor of London and achieved his lasting fame some three weeks before his death in 1770; this was when he answered George III back, after the King had somewhat curtly refused to consider a petition relating to the Middlesex elections. All 244 words of Beckford's speech are engraved on the pedestal of his statue in the Guildhall. After the marriage of his heir, William Beckford the younger, 'England's wealthiest son' and builder of the Gothick Fonthill, the house remained the home of his mother, Maria, who brought up his two daughters here, his wife having died within four years of their wedding. His mother, whom he pictured unflatteringly as Carathis in his novel *Vathek*, had 'methodistical' leanings and Beckford once wrote that he had not 'a fine Bible to spare after the West End fashion'. The house remained with the Beckford family until 1812 and was again connected with the family from 1838–41 when Beckford's son-in-law, General James Orde, was the occupant here with his second wife. General Orde was visited here in the early years of her reign by the young Queen Victoria. Beck-

5. *The West End House (ex Hall) twelve acre estate,* from the sales catalogue of 1889.

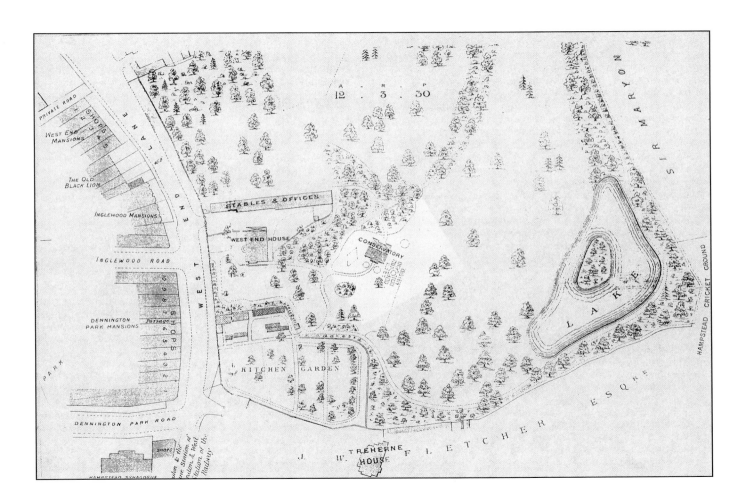

ford always came up to London for the season, even when he was very old. It was recorded then that he would occasionally ride up the Edgware Road to Hampstead and stop to 'gaze upon the old family habitation'. The final residents of West End House included Colonel Henry Cavendish, Admiral of the Fleet Sir George Sartorius and Daniel Harvey, who founded the *Sunday Times* and who, like Leigh Hunt and others, was once imprisoned for libelling George IV. After Harvey's departure in 1857, the mansion was ignominiously used for a few years as a Girls' Laundry Training School. In 1860 the North London Line was opened behind the house and in 1868 the Midland Railway crossed in front. On the OS map of that date, West End House is still standing, flush against the south side of the beginnings of Iverson Road (*q.v.*) and then, about 1871, it was pulled down. For many years a hawthorn, an elm and a horse-chestnut remained beside the roadway at this point, the only reminders of past tranquility.

This section of West End Lane is now mostly given over to the railways. Within a hundred yards or so are three **stations**. The Midland Line station, opened under the name West End in 1871, was the precursor of the new residential development, which in its turn caused the two other lines to establish stations here, the Metropolitan (now Jubilee) in 1879 and the Hampstead Junction (now North London) Line in 1888. A terrace of shops once called Cheapside was demolished in 1979 when the Bedford-St Pancras (or Bed-Pan) Line was electrified. However, a few of the old coal merchants' offices have survived. The nicely gabled West Hampstead Tube Station incorporates an estate agency founded by Ernest Owers in 1879.

Two narrow **footpaths** start hereabouts. One, next to the Midland station, wanders westward in search of Brooms-leigh Street, and another goes east through the railway wastelands to Finchley Road. The latter has a link with Priory Road across the railway, following the line of a very old right of way from Hampstead to Kilburn. The steps at the Broadhurst Gardens end of the **bridge** were once known as Granny Drippen's stairs, after one of the last of the local crossing sweepers, who used to sit there. The bridge was recently found to be seriously corroded and was threatened with closure but, prompted by the local MP, Sir Geoffrey Finsberg, London Regional Transport agreed to repair it – at a cost of some £300,000. Tucked between the tracks here is **BLACKBURN ROAD**, named in 1869 possibly after the builder, William Blackburn, who was busy locally at the time. The cobbled road leads to a straggle of depots and to the recently evacuated works at **No. 11** of Joseph Sloper and Co., makers of perforating machines since 1872. Their name can partly be read on the buildings at the rear of the terrace. **No. 3** was occupied in turn by a builder's yard, a sawmill, a bicycle maker, a pill maker and from *c*1939 by the Alliance Plating Works. Part of the bicycle maker's advertisement can still be read on the side of the house, including 'Repairs Promptly Executed. Riding Lessons Given'.

There was a tradition that West End Lane owed its winding route to its having been originally a path through the forests that bordered the old Roman Watling Street: or later it may have wound its way round plots of land. However, its twisting course and the abundance of its architectural styles make the Lane south of this point interesting and reflect the varying tastes of the Victorians and their successors. On the corner of Broadhurst Gardens, the **Railway Tavern** has spattered its Victorian solidity with jade green. Originally called the Railway Hotel (the name is still shown on the north side), it opened in early 1881 and, according to the *Kilburn Times*, was 'shortly to be furnished for the accommodation of railway travellers'. The handsomely restored **No. 90** was the local police station from 1882 to 1972, when business was transferred to Fortune Green Road. Opposite, **No. 169** shows its date 'AD 1882'. **No. 167** was until recently the home of the composer, Oliver Knussen, noted for his fantasy opera *Where The Wild Things Are.* Across the road at **No. 86** are the new premises of the Acol Bridge Academy (see Acol Road). **Nos. 80–88** are attractive detached houses with snaky-edged barge boards and imposing porches. At **No. 74** is the lively Czech Club, which opened in the mid–1950s as the Czechoslovak Colony Club: it has served as a social centre for two generations of Czech exiles.

To the right, behind **Nos. 99–145**, were once the grounds of Oaklands Hall, which was previously a smaller house called York Villa. This five-acre plot was part of a forty-acre purchase in 1822 of land between West End Lane and Kilburn High Road by Samuel Ware, an architect best known for the Burlington Arcade. The villa was built in 1826 by Charles Spain, a rich Marylebone butcher, and subsequently occupied by Francis Truefitt, 'the greatest of all barbers' (Baines) with a salon in Bond Street, where his name is still found, and by Charles Asprey, the jeweller, whose shop has also thrived in Bond Street from 1847 to the present. Another famous West End shopkeeper, Donald Nicoll, the outfitter, took over the house in 1860, but this time from Regent Street and his name survived there only until 1950. Nicoll also built houses in the Vale of Health, including the

vast Tavern, and speculated in the Metropolitan Railway Extension, of which he was a founding director with A.C. Sherriff. Nicoll Road was the original name of the local Sherriff Road. The final occupant of this property, which boasted a vinery, a glasshouse and an ice well, was the diplomat and author, Sir Charles Murray. His many achievements included the shipping of the first hippopotamus to London Zoo in 1850. The Oaklands estate was redeveloped in 1882 by the United Land Company and sold off in building plots along four new roads, Hemstal, Dynham, Cotleigh and Kingsgate. For many years **No. 141** was a Home for Unmarried Mothers and **No. 139** a private school, St Winifred's. **Nos. 121–125** have round bay windows with interesting Renaissance-style decoration, while **Nos. 113–119** are heavily swagged with fruit and fearsome faces. The council flats across the road, **Sidney Boyd Court**, are named after an Honorary Freeman of the Borough of Hampstead, also Mayor throughout the last war and an eminent surgeon at Hampstead General Hospital (see plaque). Built in 1953 on a site cleared by a flying bomb, the flats were the first post-war municipal housing development. Another large block, **King's Gardens** (1897), marks the site of The Chimes, built by E.W. Pugin in 1868 for John Rogers Herbert RA but rapidly pulled down after the artist's death in 1890. Herbert, who had previously lived at 22 Church Row, is famous for his murals in the Peers' Robing Room in the Palace of Westminster. **Kingswood Court** was built in 1935 on the site of a house called Quex Lodge. (For the southern end of West End Lane, see Section Three.)

WEST OF THE LANE

The area to the west of West End Lane, bounded by **HEM-STAL ROAD, LOWFIELD ROAD** and **SHERRIFF ROAD** was originally called the West End Park Estate. (For roads to the south, see Section Three.) In 1878 the Metropolitan Board of Works gave permission to Messrs Sherriff and Jacob to build the estate on behalf of the London Permanent Building Society. This was the year in which the Metropolitan Line was extended onwards from Finchley Road, so making this estate more easily accessible from central London. The land had previously been bought by Donald Nicoll of nearby Oaklands Hall (*q.v.*), who quickly laid out Sherriff Road with an eye to increasing his compensation claims from the railways. There is no overall pattern for the street naming on the estate. Lowfield and Hemstal were names of fields upon which the estate was built, hemstal being also a local name for a farmstead. (The 1762 estate map shows 'Hemstalls' and the 1842 Tithe Map gives 'Hempstall'.) **GLADYS ROAD** may commemorate a builder's better half. **HILLTOP ROAD** is purely descriptive, and **KYLEMORE ROAD** only suggests the builders had connections with Galway.

Houses were under construction in 1879 (*VCH*) but many seem not to have been completed until the late 1880s. The making-up of the roads was finished in 1887, but in that

year, after a child had died of fever in Lowfield Road, there were already reports to the Vestry of defective plumbing and an absence of dustbins. Many of the houses have attractive decorative features. Hemstal has pots of flowers round doorways. Gladys has handsome porch tiles. Kylemore is rich in rosettes. Sherriff Road has much to admire on **Nos. 24–36**, including barley-sugar window columns. In Hemstal Road **Beacon House** commemorates a curious building at the corner with West End Lane designed about 1880 by its owner, Charles Clarke, to look like a ruined coastal beacon. It succumbed to **St James's Mansions** in 1894. Current residents in this road include the Chess Grandmaster, Nigel Short, who at the age of 23, reached the final of the World Championships in 1988. In 1885 Alfred Harmsworth occupied one of his several West Hampstead abodes at **No. 37** Sherriff Road, where he shared lodgings with the writer, Max Pemberton. He left the following year with some reluctance, as his future wife lived round the corner, but duty called him to Coventry to edit *Bicycling News*. **No. 17** was the Institute of Occult Social Science in the late 1930s.

Also in Sherriff Road is the redbrick **St James's Church**, built in 1887 by Sir Arthur Blomfield. This distinguished architect, whose other local churches include St Mark's in

Marylebone Road and All Saints, Highgate, was a popular church builder and restorer, partly because he 'excelled in the charitable but unremunerative art of keeping down the cost' and partly because he firmly believed that churches should not impose mortification on their congregations. Blomfield had already designed the St James's Mission House in Netherwood Street in 1881, from which the congregation migrated four years later to an iron church on the Sherriff Road site. While the present church was being built to seat a thousand people, services were held in the West Hampstead Town Hall (*q.v.*). A notable feature of St James's is its eighteenth-century life-size figure of its patron saint, possibly of Spanish origin. Opposite the church, two bow-fronted houses joined by an ornate arch are labelled **West Hampstead Studios**. Of the many artists working, or at least living, here from the 1880s onwards, only one, Walter West, seems to have reached the Tate Gallery. But several exhibited at the Royal Academy, such as the twin brothers, Maurice and Edward Detmold, animal and bird painters who illustrated *The Jungle Book*, and Anna Airy, author of *The Art of Pastel*. Among recent artists here was the sculptor Paul Harnam, one-time pupil of Rodin and a founder member of the Free German League of Culture. The studios are now approached through an attractive leafy vestibule.

North of the railways, the close-packed pocket of roads between West End Lane and Sumatra Road was filled in from 1877 until the turn of the century. Many were developed by the Potter family, who owned the local foundry, and **SUMATRA ROAD** was one of the first of these. Nobody has identified the Indonesian connection, reinforced by the original names of **Nos. 121–3**, Sumatra and Batavia Villas. It could even be an American connection as

6. *Alfred Harmsworth* in 1889, aged twenty.

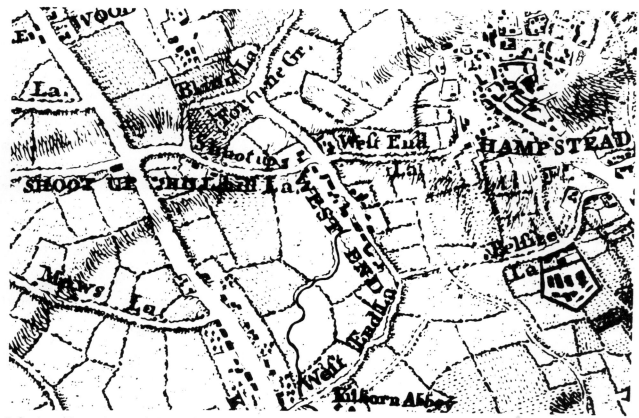

7. Section of Rocque's map of 1746, including Blind Lane in the north and Kilburn Priory in the south.

Sumatra and Batavia are also towns in the U.S.A. The street originally ran from Mill Lane to Kingdon Road but, after the destruction of Sandwell House, an extension was built to West End Lane and called Sandwell Park. Throughout 1895 the LCC battled to unite and re-number the two roads and, after a flurry of residents' petitions, supported the Sumatrans. Nos. 76–86 were bombed out of existence in the last war and the result is an official **Open Space**. The new offices at **Nos. 105–9** are on the site of Cornwall Motors, makers of three-wheeled invalid cars. **No. 141** was the home of the landscape artist, Alfred Glendinning junior, in the 1890s and **No. 98**, with a studio window, that of engraver, Dolf Rieser, in the 1980s. **Victoria Mansions** were built in the 1890s and bought by Camden Council in 1973. The houses in the northern stretch are noticeably more decorated with fancy foliage than the others but much of the road is happily sprinkled with silver birches.

SANDWELL CRESCENT was built over the grounds of Sandwell House in 1897. The garden of the house embraced part of the old West End House estate, including the grand entrance, with its two lodges, which stood where Sandwell Crescent meets West End Lane. The name may have a connection with the widow, Mary Sandwell, who was admitted as a tenant of Hampstead manor in 1800.

The dividing line between the grounds of Sandwell House and Lauriston Lodge is roughly shown by **KINGDON ROAD**. The Lodge was a large house built about 1800 by Germain Lavie *q.v.*) and later occupied by Sir William Woods, Garter King-at-Arms: he died in 1842 and was reputedly the last person to be buried inside the Parish Church. Mrs Adeline Barnes believed she was the granddaughter of two of his servants. She records the house as being of red brick with a fine entrance and some stained glass windows. It was demolished in 1892 when the area was developed. The road name may be linked with Emmeline Kingdon, a spinster of Bath, who speculated in several local building schemes around 1881 when this road was built. Two artists of note were living here in the 1890s – the sculptor George McCulloch at **No. 30** and the stained glass artist, John Clement Bell, at **No. 27**: his firm Clayton and Bell made the windows in the Parish Church and his family is buried in the Churchyard (see *Buried in Hampstead*).

A contemporary development was **DENNINGTON PARK ROAD**, which follows the line of an old path known locally as Sweetbriar Walk: this led past Lauriston Lodge and headed for Brondesbury. Dennington is the name of villages in Devon, Suffolk and Yorkshire, but no local connection has been found. **No. 34** still bears its date (1882) and its old name, Grosvenor House. At the turn of the century, this was Grosvenor School and there were other schools at **No. 11** and **No. 7**, which was the Dennington College for Girls. About the same period, the artist George Goodwin Kilburne was living at **No. 24**: he began his career as an engraver, apprenticed to the Dalziel Brothers of Camden Town, one of whose daughters he married. The television actor, Michael Elphick, lived at **No. 37** in the 1980s. **Dene Mansions** are a reminder of the large house called Little Dene which stood here from 1832 to 1904 and was the home of the land-owning Ripley family. The octagonal **Hampstead Synagogue** was built on the site of Lauriston Lodge and opened in 1892. Founder members included Joseph (Lord) Duveen and a lawyer, Herbert Bentwich, who brought in his brother-in-law-, Delissa Joseph, an architect. Joseph, also responsible for the original Piccadilly Tube Station, added an extension in 1901, when the con-

gregation had grown to be the largest in the United Synagogue. This is now a Listed Building, described as having
an 'eclectic French Gothic/Romanesque style'. Though an
Orthodox Synagogue, with the usual segregation of the
sexes, both the architect and the early congregation intro-
duced liberal ideas in the layout of the building and the
form of service. As in any Synagogue, there are no repre-
sentations of God or the human form, but there are several
striking groups of symbolic stained glass. A complete history of the Synagogue, which now includes a Community
Centre added by Seifert in 1964, has been written by a
recent minister, Raymond Apple. A back entrance from
West End Lane has attractive wrought iron. The high-tech
Spiro Garage houses a centre for Jewish studies.

The **West Hampstead Branch Library**, after being
bombed out of Westbere Road and seeking shelter in Mill
Lane, came to its present building in 1954. The foundation
stone records that Councillor G. Finsberg (later Hampstead's MP) was Chairman of the Public Libraries Committee at the time. One author unlikely to be represented here
is Sarah Doudney, who lived in a house on this site, Gothic
Lodge, just before it was demolished in 1882: her romantic
fiction has been labelled 'rather Mills and Boon'. Other
houses and shops on this corner were demolished by
bombing in 1944, when an entire wedding party was wiped
out (see *Hampstead at War*).

HOLMDALE, **GLENBROOK** and **INGLEWOOD
ROADS** evidently got names at random from the country-
lovers' list. **Welbeck Mansions**, erected in Inglewood Road
in 1897, are no country cottages but notable for their fancy
ironwork balconies. The flats are built on the site of Potter's
foundry (*q.v.*) which did much work for the Duke of Portland at Welbeck Abbey; hence, perhaps, the name of the

mansions. The south side of the road marks the site of
Potter's home, Poplar House, which was originally a small
eighteenth-century building called the White House. This
was enlarged about 1800 by Josiah Boydell, an eminent
painter and engraver, who lived here from 1783–1808.
Boydell exhibited at the Royal Academy between 1772 and
1799 and took an active part in local life. In 1848–9 Poplar
House unexpectedly became a monastery – the home of
Father Dominic Barberi and the Passionists. This was a
Roman Catholic Order devoted to missionary work and
their mission here was to Irish workers. The Potter family
took over the house in 1851 and stayed until shortly before
its demolition in 1891. Many of the present houses here
display dragons or sunflowers, or other architectural
whims. The builder was Jabez Reynolds of Holmdale Road
and most were erected in 1883–4. **Holmdale Mansions**
were built in 1904. **INGLEWOOD MEWS**, originally Dennington Park Mews in the 1896 Directory and changed in
1903, housed a riding master and a vet's shoeing forge in
Edwardian times. The **garages** mark the old entrance to the
foundry. Glenbrook Road was likened to a quagmire in its
early days and was not made up until 1890. **SOLENT
ROAD**, started in 1877, presumably once had connections
with the Isle of Wight area. The stretch south of Glenbrook
Road was called Solent Crescent until 1892. The same
bombs which gave Sumatra Road an Open Space gave this
road room for a **Family Health Clinic** (since enlarged) on
the site of Nos. 9–17. Most of the roads in this area have
houses which are neat but not gaudy though Solent Road
specialises in sprightly icing sugar decor round its doors
and windows.

The names of **PANDORA** and **NARCISSUS ROADS**
were probably designed to blind the original housebuyers

with Greek mythology, but Pandora was also the name of a three-master which made two daring attempts to find the North West Passage in 1875/6, just before the road was built. Alfred Harmsworth, the future master of mass circulation, was one of the first residents of Pandora Road. Newly married at Hampstead Parish Church, he moved into **No. 31** with his wife Mary in 1888. The rent was £26 per annum, which was all he could afford. Their neighbours included an architect, an artist and a builder, not up to his wife's social pretensions, and later Viscount Northcliffe would not willingly discuss his years in Pandora Road. Yet, partly from his attic here, crowned with a curly lightning conductor, he launched his first successful magazine, *Answers*. In 1890, with his brother Harold, he founded the Pandora Publishing Company, which gave birth to *Comic Cuts* and other popular papers. By the following year, Harmsworth no longer needed to walk the four miles to his office but had his secretary bring his work out to Pandora Road; and from this West Hampstead terrace he moved to a mansion near Broadstairs. A blue plaque to Lord Northcliffe was erected on No. 31 in 1979 and it remains the only blue plaque in NW6. **No. 7** was long the home of a journalist, Philip Layman, who ran the Herbal Research Centre here in the 1930s. He achieved some notoriety by being fined ten pounds for having an illicit still, which was in fact old banana skins in an oilcan. This house is one of several in the road which has kept its original stained glass.

The small enclave of **BROOMSLEIGH, RAVENSHAW, GLASTONBURY** and **DORNFELL STREETS** can be entered only from Mill Lane. This triangular estate is so shaped and isolated because it was built on a piece of land cut off from the Earlsfield Estate by the Midland Railway. It was developed in 1881 by the Land Building Investment and Cottage Improvement Co. Ltd. and somehow it never became connected up even with the streets to the east, although there is a footpath beside the railway line. The names were probably invented deliberately to attract customers, though Glastonbury may have a Somerset connection and Broomsleigh is a country seat in West Kent. It is hard to account for these four 'streets' amongst the surrounding 'roads'; they consist mainly of small terraced houses in varying styles. At **No. 15** Ravenshaw Street there is an unusual, heart-shaped stone plaque commemorating Elizabeth Hagedorn, who lived there from 1892 to 1945. She had no claim to national fame but her family, who erected the plaque, considered her a famous mother. The **Community Hall** was opened in Broomsleigh Street as Emmanuel Church's Mission Hall in 1903 and sold by the church in 1979 for residential use. After much fighting and fund-raising (some £48,000) and refurbishment, a new Community Hall was opened here in 1981 and completed in 1983. The BBC contributed to the restoration by repainting the walls during their filming of the series *Fanny by Gaslight* at the hall. The little estate is dominated by the four storeys of the **Beckford Primary School**, whose entrance is in Dornfell Street, although it was first known as the Broomsleigh Street School. The enlargement was completed in 1891, and its new name, adopted about 1933, commemorates the Beckford family who were once the pride of old West End. There are now some 450 pupils in the school and 43 ethnic-minority groups, something of a record.

THE POWELL-COTTON ESTATE

The history of what became known as the Powell-Cotton Estate is a long one and its origins are bound up with the Shutt-up or Shotuppe Hill Estate to the east of the present Shoot-up Hill. The meaning of the name has not been unravelled, though there are the usual theories that Henry VIII came out here to shoot up the game in the Forest of Middlesex.

The original Shutt-up Hill Estate had been parcelled out of the manorial lands held by the abbots of Westminster. In 1312 it was run by the Knights Templar (though Park says that the ownership was disputed) and when their Order was dissolved it passed to the Knights Hospitaller of St John of Jerusalem, who held the estate and Abbey Farm (see Section Three) until the Dissolution of the Monasteries. By this time the estate was called the Manor of Shutt-up Hill (and sometimes the Manor of Hampstead), it being a practice of religious foundations to elevate their farms and lands to 'manors' to enable them to claim special privileges.

At the Dissolution, the estate passed to Sir Roger Cholmley, Chief Baron of the Exchequer, and through his daughter, in 1595, to Sir Arthur Attye, Secretary to the Earl of Leicester and Public Orator at Oxford. After changing hands a number of times, the freehold of Shutt-up Hill Farm was bought in 1773 by John Powell of Fulham, a secretary to George III and one-time Paymaster General. Four years later he also acquired the Thanet estate of Charles James Fox, including the stately home of Quex Park; but his descendants came to live in Hampstead, including another John Powell, who owned Heath Lodge near Jack Straw's Castle and was a front-line fighter in the battle to save the Heath for the public.

In 1838 Shoot-up Hill and its farm were inherited by Captain Henry Cotton from his maternal uncle. When not on duty with the Bengal Cavalry, Captain Cotton lived at Kingsgate in Kent, not far from the Powells. His inheritance also included the West End Lane Estate, described later, and the two properties were known as the Powell-Cotton Estates. Plans were drawn up to develop the northern section in 1855 but building was delayed until the 1870s because of uncertainty about where the railway lines would be laid.

The extent of the Shoot-up Hill Estate can be seen by the length of the present **FORDWYCH ROAD**. Like so many roads on Powell-Cotton land, this was named after a place in north-east Kent, actually spelled Fordwich. The road was developed gradually from the 1870s and completed only by 1899. Some of the houses have nicely decorated facades, such as **Nos. 37** and **39** and **Nos. 65** and **67** with Viking and other faces. A grander road than those to the south, its residents at the turn of the century included a surgeon, two doctors, a barrister and three solicitors. There was also a ladies' seminary and at **No. 57** another school, Stanwell House. **No. 10** was the home from 1930–33 of one of the country's foremost Cubists and Vorticists, David Bomberg. A founder member of the London Group, his exuberant work is much visible on the walls of the Tate Gallery. He later lived in Lymington Road, Greville Place, Rosslyn Hill and Steele's Road. In Edwardian times, two other artists lived in this road, Isobel Hutchinson, portraitist, at **No. 43**, and Katharine Johnson, flower painter, at **No. 66**. The new low-profile **St Cuthbert's Church** was designed by Jeremy Allen and consecrated in 1988. Together with the adjoining **Davina House**, purpose-built sheltered flats for the elderly, it stands on the site of the old church, consecrated in 1887, and incorporates some of its features. These include part of the chancel window, a foundation stone of 1903 and the old church bell, which stands at the entrance. One of the windows in the new church has been dedicated to Miss Coldstream, sister of Sir William, the eminent painter (see below), who worshipped here.

St Cuthbert's has had a difficult history. The first temporary building fell victim to the Midland Railway and its successor was hit by a fire bomb in the last war. Both the church and the adjoining church hall were so dilapidated by 1985 that they had to be demolished.

Going north up this section of the Powell-Cotton Estate, all in NW2, a number of short roads lead off Fordwych Road to the left. The first is **GARLINGE ROAD**, another Kentish name, approved in 1880. The early houses were

8. *Major Powell-Cotton*, the big game hunter, *c*1908, from a portrait by R.H. Miller.

9. *David Bomberg*, self-portrait, *c*1932.

called by such grand names as Belsize Lodge, Ardenlea, Uffculme, Clarence House and Claremont Lodge. **No. 10**, called Marlborough House, was the home of the Coldstream family from 1910 until the late 1930s. The father was a popular local doctor and the youngest of his five children was (Sir) William (1908–1987) who became a well-known artist and Slade Professor of Fine Art at University College, London: he founded the Euston Road School of artists and wrote influential reports on art education. He later lived in Belsize Park and Cannon Hill.

The prefab **Garlinge Cottages** were built for a nursery school and opened in 1990. The area opposite was shattered by a flying bomb in the last war and now holds council houses, such as **Chevington**. **ST CUTHBERT'S ROAD**, named in the 1880s after the nearby church, was formerly called Dent de Lion Road, a surprisingly Kentish name. There are some attractive houses here – **Nos. 1–11** with scrolled bay windows and **Nos. 13–23** with their old numbers over the door: the tympani are decorated, in some cases with naked ladies. On a bomb site opposite, **Nos. 8** and **10** are pleasantly hipped-roofed, white-washed and pebble-dashed. The silver-birched crescent, **KINGSCROFT ROAD**, a late development, is on the site of Shootup Hill Farm. By the 1830s the farm buildings were evidently attached to an imposing residence called The Elms, once thought to have been the residence in 1834 of the writer, Harrison Ainsworth (cf: Ainsworth Estate). Recent research, however, has shown that Ainsworth stayed at Elm Lodge on the west side of the High Road (on the site of the State Cinema) and it was there that he wrote the successful *Rookwood*, which popularised the fiction of Dick Turpin's ride to York. By 1873, The Elms had become Kingsgate Lodge, named after Colonel Cotton's Kentish seat. Kingsgate had already been used for a local road by the time the present houses were built in 1912/13, so Kingscroft was presumably a compromise. Some of the old farm buildings did not disappear until early this century. To the south of The Elms was Royston Hall, previously Ripley's Farm and Prospect Farm. The Brawne family were living here in 1786 and widow Brawne and her daughter Fanny remained until 1802, after which they moved to Hampstead and the world of Keats.

MANSTONE ROAD, spelt differently from the village in Kent, is a road of pleasant Victorian villas. The Directories show that the south-east side was developed in 1899 and the north-west side two years later. **No. 10** is now the Marie Stopes Nursing Home. **RONDU ROAD** and **SKARDU ROAD**, built up between 1890 and 1900, are named after places in Kashmir visited by Major Percy Powell-Cotton. The major was a grandson of Colonel Cotton and inherited the estates in 1894. A big-game hunter, naturalist and anthropologist, he bagged and stuffed a large number of animals on his expeditions and these can still be seen in the Powell-Cotton Museum at Quex Park. **Rondu House** has bagged the site of the Cricklewood Presbyterian Church.

With **EBBSFLEET ROAD**, christened in 1893, and **RICHBOROUGH ROAD** we are back among the Kentish names. This is the north-west corner of Hampstead, on the boundaries defined in tenth-century charters and exactly adopted by the nineteenth-century Boundary Commission. One of these original boundaries ran from Hampstead North End to Watling Street, where the Moeurburn crossed the road. Near this spot in Anglo-Saxon times was a pool where women would be ducked as a punishment for 'transgressing against the peace of their households and

the credit of the community'. The culprit was tied to a chair suspended from a beam and ducked as many times as the sentence directed.

At the west end is Cricklewood Broadway, which soon becomes **SHOOT-UP HILL**, an old name (see above) given new meaning by modern traffic. The name appears on Rocque's map of 1746 but was not officially approved until 1899, when the road was being newly developed. Some of those substantial old houses still stand at the southern end, built for surgeons and solicitors and other eminent Victorians. But the roadway itself, being the Roman Watling Street, leading from Dover to Chester via London and St Albans, must be noted here as the oldest street or half-street in Hampstead. In the late 1930s, the musical Max Jaffa was living at **Hillcrest Court** with, next door, the Collins family, including daughters Jackie and Joan, later known as writer, and actress, respectively. To the south, **Templar House**, commemorating the Knights Templar, originated in 1939 but was complicated by the flying bomb of 1944. The development, covering nearly three and a half acres, was finally completed in 1954 and opened by Princess Anne.

MINSTER ROAD takes us back to Thanet and across the Midland Railway. The road's main interest is that at the east end it follows the track of the old Blind Lane (*q.v.*), shown on the earliest maps of the area. Behind the houses at the east end can be seen the old trees of the cemetery and the spire of one of the chapels. At the other end, **Nos. 2** and **4** were originally named the Bosphorus and Esperanza respectively, but the former soon changed to Mount Ephraim. **SARRE ROAD** and **WESTBERE ROAD** also have Kentish derivations and were developed at the turn of the century. At the junction of these two roads, two new

West Hampstead Library.

10. The original *West Hampstead Library*, at the junction of Sarre Road and Westbere Road.

houses have been built on the site of the West Hampstead (originally West End) Branch Library, which operated here from 1901 to 1940, when it was destroyed by a fire bomb. The branch wandered in several directions thereafter before settling in Dennington Park Road.

At the north end of Westbere Road, before it crosses the borough boundary and changes its name, is **Hampstead School**. In 1961 this large comprehensive took over and added to buildings used by Haberdashers' Aske's School, based here between 1898 and 1961. The self-confident coat of arms of the ancient Haberdashers' Company remains in a prominent position on the buildings with its injunction to 'Serve and Obey'. The nearby **No. 80** was until recently the

home of Sir Geoffrey Finsberg, Conservative MP for Hampstead, 1970–92. On the west side of the road, next to the Midland Line, is **Westcroft Close**, a council estate. This title originally applied to some adjoining prefabricated houses, given by the American Government after the last war. Designed to last ten years, the prefabs were only recently demolished. Also by the railway is the **Westbere Copse**, a one-acre nature reserve, which boasts foxes and rabbits and a wheelchair path, built in 1989 by an international group of students. Just across the border in Hendon is a Hampstead enclave, the **Westcroft Estate**, with streets named after Galsworthy, Besant and other Hampstead worthies. This was built by Hampstead Council in 1934 to house an overflow of residents who were allowed to retain some of their Hampstead status: they could, for instance, buy graves in the local cemetery at parishioners' rates. Residents were recently paying rent to Camden and poll tax to Barnet but a Boundary Commission proposal to include all the estate in Camden met with stiff opposition. **Kent Hall** commemorates the opening of the estate by the Duke of Kent in 1935: his son, the present Duke, planted a tree here in 1985 to mark its jubilee. Westcroft was originally a Hendon farm, which in the 1890s became a Home of Rest for Horses, a charity (still extant) to help the working poor with their working animals.

The remaining roads on this part of the Powell-Cotton estate were developed somewhat later and given the exotic names, approved in 1901, of **SOMALI ROAD**, **MENELIK ROAD**, **ASMARA ROAD** and **GONDAR GARDENS**. These names commemorate further places in East Africa frequented by the intrepid Major Powell-Cotton, except Menelik which was the name of the Emperor who defeated the Italians in Abyssinia in 1896. The Powell-Cotton

Museum at Quex Park includes some sacred paintings saved from Gondar when that ancient city was sacked by the Dervishes in 1887. Development of the roads was delayed by worry over the local cemetery plans but Somali Road was mainly built up by 1910, Menelik by 1926 and Asmara by 1928. As the proximity of the cemetery became more welcome (see Agamemnon Road) the houses became more expensive. Alan Coren devoted one of his *Times* columns to Menelik Road, noting 'the houses have not only unnecessarily sturdy walls to keep out the sun and inappropriate balconies to take advantage of it, they have little turrets and crenellations and embrasures, as if in anticipation of assault. It has often occurred to me that, if one were ever called up to defend Cricklewood to the death, Menelik Road would be the place to take one's stand.' Among those now living in Somali Road is Andrew Roth, political correspondent and author of *Parliamentary Profiles* (recreations in *Who's Who* – sketching and jazz-dancing).

In Asmara Road is Professor Joseph Rotblat, the nuclear physicist who helped to develop the first atom bomb: he is now a disarmament campaigner and president of Pugwash, the international scientists' organisation. And in Gondar Gardens is Doris Lessing, distinguished author of *The Grass is Singing* and thirty other books. The first mention of Gonder [*sic*] Gardens is in the 1894/5 Directory, but it was 1910 before the full plan had been realised, with fairly spacious and comfortable houses. The development encircled the six-million gallon **reservoir** which in 1866 had been bought by the West Middlesex Waterworks from the Grand Junction Company. Later known as the Shoot-up Hill Reservoir, it is 323 feet above sea level and now belongs to Thames Water. South of **St Elmo Mansions**, a path used to emerge from alongside the reservoir and link this part of Hampstead with Child's Hill. It can still be traced through the cut down to Sarre Road, along Somali, across Menelik and past the University College School playing fields. This is **Hocroft Walk**, an ancient right of way, which ends up at Farm Avenue and Farm Walk, Older local residents happily remember playing here when the fields belonged to 'Daddy Dickens'.

THE MILL LANE AREA

Opposite the junction of Shoot-up Hill and Mill Lane, on the west side, is the site of an old windmill, nearly marked by a vast block of flats called **Windmill Court**. The mill, which was probably more used than the other local ones in Hampstead Village because the approach was less steep, lasted until 1861 when, so it was said, a gale blew the sails round with such ferocity that the friction caused a fire which burnt the mill down.

MILL LANE is one of the earliest roads in the area. Previous names of various stretches included on the south side Midland Cottages (near the railway) and Howard Terrace and, on the north side, Westbere Villas and Watts Cottages. The whole road was once known as Windmill Hill Lane or Shoot-up Hill Lane, but maps of the 1860s give Mill Lane as an alternative name, and this was finally approved in 1899. Opposite Midland Cottages there were farm buildings, including cowsheds and haystacks, until 1890.

Nos. 2–18 were for a long time known as Fordwych Crescent. The covered passage by the railway, next to No. 18, is called **Wayne Kirkum Way** to commemorate a teenager who was killed on the railway near here in 1984 (see plaque): the way leads to Brassey Road (see below). Across the railway, the high-rise **Ellerton** has replaced the railway

cottages and the **Alliance Tavern** (date plaque – 1886) has changed its frontage: its signboard used to show the alliance of Wellington and Blücher but now features two anonymous cavaliers. For most of this century, **No. 50** was a butcher's and **No. 54** a watchmaker's. The former has become an art gallery but No. 54 is unchanged. Clifford Bowler took over the Clock House in 1923, when he 'looked across the street at fields where horses grazed' and, though over 90, he still works a six-day week, sitting in his shop window. For many years an Express Dairy, **No. 62** has happily become the **West Hampstead Community Centre** since 1972. A wide range of useful services and courses can be found here, including (expectedly) counselling and Karate and (unexpectedly) a Bengali language and dance class. The Centre, mostly run by volunteers, is also active at the Hall in Broomsleigh Street and the charity (jumble) shop at **No. 92**. **No. 100** shows its original name of Downshire House and its date, 1884 but, like many others in this street, the bottom half does not belong to the top. Further east, **Nos. 41–83** are still labelled The Pavement, 1888. Sadly, many of the useful shops in the Lane have given way to offices and so many were empty in 1989 that the new name of Mortuary Lane was suggested.

By **Cavendish Mansions**, a passageway leads to a large

11. *Mill Lane*, early this century.

12. *The windmill* at the Shoot-up Hill end of Mill Lane.

open space, currently a play centre. At the end of the last century, this held the Priory Tennis Club, of which the ubiquitous Alfred Harmsworth (*q.v.*) was a notable member. It was then developed as the London General Omnibus Company stables. These, together with the omnibus depot, were built about 1895 and housed up to seventy horses. From here, some horse buses went to Elephant & Castle, more or less on the lines of the 159 bus, while others trod the route of the future 28 bus to Fulham Road. Just after the turn of the century, horses gave way to trams and the site was later used as a Post Office garage.

On the opposite side of the road, **Cholmley Gardens** was built on the site of a large property with a lake and winding paths in its grounds. This was Cholmley Lodge, presum-ably named after the one-time owner of the Shoot-up Hill Estate, who was also the founder of Highgate School. There was a house on this site in 1762 but the Lodge was built in 1814 and much enlarged afterwards. The owner in 1845 was Dr Herbert Evans, who had earlier counted John Constable among his patients and had his portrait painted by him. The last owner was Captain Henry Notman, once Managing Director of the Southern Indian Railway and,

13. *Emmanuel School* in 1844, drawn by its architect, Charles Miles. On the right is Cholmley Lodge.

nine years after he left in 1914, the house was demolished – the last of the big houses in West Hampstead. At first the land was developed only on the perimeter of the estate, leaving large private gardens in the middle. One of the last sections to be erected was that at the corner with West End Lane. This part has been used in its time as a bank, as another temporary home for the West Hampstead Branch Library (until 1954) and as a WVS Centre. The Russian-born artist, Naum Gabo, a leading light in constructivist art, lived at **No. 101** Cholmley Gardens between 1938 and 1946. His kinetic sculpture now livens up the Tate. Present residents include the travel writer, once called 'England's greatest pedestrian', John Hillaby, Jonathan Speelman, one of the area's two Chess Grandmasters, and other current attractions include the air raid shelters, which have sur-

vived from the last war. The block to the west of the school marks the site of a small Mission Church erected in 1875. Ten years later it was doubled in size and was in heavy demand until Emmanuel Church (*q.v.*) was built on West End Green in 1898.

In 1845 what is now **Emmanuel School** consisted of one classroom and a cottage for the mistress, which had been erected on one tenth of an acre of land. Part of the orchard of Cholmley Lodge was donated and the whole plot was enfranchised by Sir Thomas Maryon Wilson, the Lord of the Manor. When it was built it was Hampstead's smallest Church School and it was launched by the Parish Church so that the children of West End, who found their daily school journey such uphill work, would not miss their 'pious exercises and the godly discipline of labour'. The first building was designed by Charles Miles of the West End Hall family. For economy's sake, it cost only £585, including the schoolmistress's cottage. To start with there was accommodation for 143 children and the building allowed them only six square feet of space each. Apart from the mullioned windows, most of Miles's work has disappeared. By 1872 the local population had grown so much that the teacher complained that she was having to give lessons in her own private kitchen. The buildings were enlarged then and again in 1892, when the crenellated doorway was added – and still stands – bearing the watchword 'Early will I seek Thee'. This was not the school's only way of encouraging punctuality: rosettes and silver medals were awarded to those who arrived on time. In 1874 a local builder, Joseph Webb, erected the present picturesque cottage in the playground as a home for the schoolmistress. This now houses the school office and a staff room. (The diocese of London's shield is on the wall.)

There were 95 children on the roll in 1863 and 354 in 1901. Today there are over 100. Despite enlargement and re-building and a shaking by rockets during the last war, the school has retained its village atmosphere to the last and now hopes for a move to new premises across the road.

To the north of Mill Lane, **ALDRED ROAD** was de-veloped from 1868 by the Land Company of London. No explanation of the street name has been found, though someone may have recalled Aldred, Archbishop of York, who crowned the Conqueror in 1066: there had doubtless been great celebrations of this in 1866. (Another Aldred Road was built in Southwark the following year.) At the lower end St George's House loudly proclaims its name, dating from 1888. Other houses on the same side are pleasantly coated in icing sugar. A new development of town houses called **Melaris Mews**, squeezed six houses onto a quarter-acre site, which had been used by the War Office in the last war. This was originally called Orestes Mews because, said the agents, it was surrounded by the Greek Roads of West Hampstead (see below). **HILLFIELD ROAD**, built over one of the many local fields of that name, was developed by the Land Company of London at the same time. The road, part of which used to be known as Florence Villas, was completed in 1887 in uniform style, but it is a sunny, seaside style, bristling with bow win-dows, and the view of Hampstead Parish Church is stun-ning. In the 1920s, **No. 6** housed a branch of the Hamp-stead Provident Dispensary, which provided cheap medi-cine for the poor. Arthur Waugh, the publisher, lived at **No. 11**, called Dunedin, at the turn of the century. He was the father of two distinguished writers who were both born here – Alec in 1898 and Evelyn in 1903. Alec Waugh, in his *Early Years*, admits that Hillfield Road was 'not socially a

14. *Evelyn Waugh* in the 1930s, photographed by Howard Coster.

good address' and 'I doubt if one clubman in a hundred would have heard of it'. But the air was good for his father's asthma and the view of the Surrey hills from his nursery window made him feel he was in the country. All that Evelyn Waugh says of his birth in his autobiography is: 'I have no more memory of the house where this occurred than of the event itself', and he describes Hillfield Road as a 'cul-de-sac...near the Hampstead Cricket Ground off the Finchley Road'. In 1907 the Waughs built themselves a house near Hampstead's North End, but after World War I the postal address was changed to 145 North End Road, Golders Green. Anxious to maintain a fashionable postmark, Evelyn liked to take his letters up the hill to post in Hampstead.

A large gap at the east end of Hillfield Road was, until recently, filled by Berridge House. This solid building in institutional style was opened in 1871 to contain the boys' section of the Certified Industrial School, run by the Field Lane foundation. The school had its origins in the Sabbath School of 1841, founded in the appalling slums of Field Lane, near Hatton Garden. After the 1870 Education Act, it branched out into Industrial Schools and, when the Home Office decided that these must move out of London, the boys went to Berridge House and the girls to Church Row, Hampstead. The 100 boys (later 140) were trained in such trades as shoemaking, carpentry, bakery and tailoring. As Baines said at the time, 'Street arabs...rescued from the pernicious influences of their old companions...receive a training to fit them for careers of respectability and usefulness.' After the introduction of approved schools and the probation service, the numbers fell and the property was sold in 1932 to the Domestic Science College in Fortune Green Road (q.v.). This college was called Berridge House after the Irish philanthropist who provided funds for 'education in economic and sanitary services'. The last occupants of the building were Westfield College.

When in 1874 the parish picked twenty acres of land for the Hampstead Cemetery (q.v.) there were many objections from local landowners who thought that it would deter potential house purchasers. For a time the only development in the area was to the south, where **AGAMEMNON**, **AJAX**, **ACHILLES** and **ULYSSES ROADS** were built around 1886 as lower middle class terraced housing. Presumably to offset their inferior location, they were given the names of four top people from the Trojan War, though another theory suggests that one or two roads were named after battleships. Not long before the roads were being built, some of the first iron clad warships were being launched amid great public excitement. The theory was thought to have been torpedoed by the fact that the northern leg of Agamemnon Road was earlier called Penelope Road – but Penelope was also the name of a warship. The houses came slowly and the roads did not begin to fill up until the 1890s, when many realised the advantages of living in an area which was as quiet as the grave.

A major incident which occurred in this area in 1944, when eight bombs fell and killed sixteen people, explains the newish houses at **Nos. 17–31** and **49–51** Agamemnon Road. Most of the original houses in the road have ferny facades and many have decorative plaques. Of the very few houses in Ajax Road, the one at the corner with Ulysses (and numbered in that road) has a date plaque with 1888.

AROUND IVERSON ROAD

As has already been told in the West End Lane story, the arrival of the railways from 1860 meant the departure of old West End House. After a brief ignominious spell as a Girls' Laundry Training School, it was bought, along with property to the west, by the British Land Company. The building of five roads on this property by the Land Company, together with the development of Netherwood Street and Palmerston Road (*q.v.*), was significant because they were the first in the area and they set the tone for the entire district. The method of operation was for the land companies to buy up parcels of land, put down roads and sewers, and then to sell off building plots. Working alongside the land companies were the building societies, who provided money on mortgage to the house builders. In this way, cheap but respectable houses were built for the upper working class and the lower middle class. To start with, the occupiers included skilled craftsmen and some professional people but by 1898, judging by the number of lodgers to be found, the residents were less prosperous and the area was suffering from a general depression.

IVERSON ROAD, which runs right through the site of West End House, was among the first developments, and was named in 1869. The British Land Company, which later laid out the Carlile Estate in central Hampstead (see

The Streets of Hampstead), often chose names for its roads without any local or other identifiable connections and Iverson is no exception. The names of the early sections of the road were Coleridge Villas, Derbyshire Cottages, Iverson Gardens, Gilbert Terrace and Richmond Villas. Until recently the west end of the road was dominated by the ornate Brondesbury Baptist Chapel (see Kilburn High Road) with a Church Hall at **No. 9**. The Chapel has now been swept away and since 1989 the hall has been replaced by a four-storey Christian Centre including a church and flats. Back in the 1880s, C.W. Crook and Sons, Job Masters, were located at **No. 1**, offering their 'Fashionable Broughams, Clarences and Open Carriages etc.' while, at **No. 3**, Jennings Smith, Sanitary and Electrical Engineers, advertised among other services 'lightning conductors and speaking tubes fitted'. In the 1890s, **No. 2** was the Orderly Room of the Kilburn Company of London's Artillery Brigade. **Nos. 21–3** offer 'Residential Chambers' on a decorated plaque and were presumably built as a rooming house. **No. 36** on the other side has 'Winkfield House' cut over the door, possibly the name of the ladies' school here in 1885. It was in this year that Frederick Rolfe (see Broadhurst Gardens) lived somewhere in Iverson Road. Underneath the arches of the **railway bridge** (Jubilee Line)

15. *Iverson Road*, after bombing in the last war. (From *Hampstead at War*).

various light industries hum away, while above the arches the pigeons coo triumphantly, having escaped any attempts to discourage them and their droppings. Note the ornamentation on **Nos 82–4** and the forlorn **No. 136**, which also has carved heads. Nearby is an **Open Space**, a Camden Children's Play Area, originally with a plaque in memory of Jim Singleton, who cared for it from its opening in 1960 until his death in 1975. The space was created by a rocket in the last war and the **mural** by architects Tim Bruce-Dick Associates, who were working on local council projects; students from the Architectural Association did the painting.

Among the many Hampstead addresses recorded for Alfred Harmsworth is **No. 77** Iverson Road, where he lodged around 1887. His biographers have recorded that the house was a haven of aspidistras and lace curtains, and that the landlady's son became Harmsworth's first office boy. In 1890, the marine artist, Fritz Althaus, exhibitor at the Royal Academy 1887–1914, was living at **No. 85**, one of a row of houses **Nos. 75–93** with attractive decorative details. The Young Adventurers' Club at **No. 145** is described as a hostel for unsupported boys: it was opened in 1969 by Princess Anne and is labelled Finsberg House after Hampstead's MP. The pillarbox on the pavement here is Edwardian. **No. 162** opposite is still called 'Lyon House' as it was in the 1880s. From here to West End Lane, the north side of the road has stretches of cobbles and yards, which are relics of the Midland Railway's goods services and of their West End Station, opened in 1871. An old resident remembers the cattle trucks being shunted into sidings and hearing the cows mooing all night, along with the noise of wheel-tapping. By 1885 the yards held six coal merchants and two cement merchants and by 1918 also a builders'

16. Advertisements for C.W. Crook & Sons and James Crook from an 1899 Directory.

merchant and two wholesale potato merchants. Most of these commodities were still available until the early 1970s, when car repairs predominated. Today the **Hampstead Garden Centre** blooms here. Further east, two buildings called Cumberland House and Chesterfield House had arrived by 1885 and departed by 1910. One of the residents of Cumberland House in 1896 was the artist, Alfred Slocombe, previously noted on West End Green. He was one of a family of artists, including Shirley Slocombe, an RA exhibitor, who also lived at Cumberland House. The only antiquity to survive in this stretch of the road is a five-seater bench of decorative cast iron.

Opposite, at the junction with West End Lane, a complex of shops, business units and a restaurant was completed in 1990 and called **Hampstead West**. Redcroft is the name of **No. 226** and Udare House that of another part. The site next door was occupied from 1926 to 1990 by Beck and Pollitzer, exhibition contractors, who in later years also acquired the row of cottages **Nos. 202–220**. This was formerly known as Heysham Terrace and was built by the Midland Railway in 1897 for its rail-workers. After some years of decay and a threat of demolition the cottages have recently been renovated. C. Tavener and Son Ltd, builders and decorators, have had their offices and works at **No. 188** since 1935.

In 1872 John Edward Medley of St John's Wood bought a plot of land here and, when he built on it seven years later, **MEDLEY ROAD** was named after him. All the houses are of the same decorated style and some have kept their nice original railings. **No. 8A** has a square arch to its yard behind, formerly used by builders, now by pastrycooks. **No. 2** in this small cul-de-sac between Iverson Road and the North London Line used to be the office of the Registrar of Births and Deaths. A 'secret orchard' has recently been discovered between Medley Road and the North London Line: it is known as the Medley Iverson Ancient Orchard (MIAO), has walnut and cherry trees and is protected by the Ancient Orchard Association. North of Iverson Road (No. 73) is **ARIEL ROAD** which was given its present name in 1885, having been Ariel Street from 1869. The houses on the east side, all built at the same time, were originally called Spencer Terrace: they have a touch of the Gothic in their triple-arched windows. **No. 9** was St Cuthbert's Parish Room. Apart from literary allusions, Ariel is also a satellite of Uranus but this does not really explain its appearance in West Hampstead. The adjoining **LOVERIDGE ROAD** also began life in 1869, also with an inexplicable name. Overshadowed at the west end by the railway and lacking decorative features on the houses, except **Nos. 1–3** and **No. 78**, this looks one of the humbler streets of West Hampstead. **No. 37** and **No. 54** have archways, which presumably led to yards behind. **Nos. 63–5** have frontages which suggest they were once shops, and **No. 68** was for many years a grocery called Dibb. Until recently, **No. 80** was an off-licence and in the 1960s and the '70s a pub called the Wat Tyler. The railway arches house a number of businesses, mainly car repairs, but the partly cobbled **Loveridge Mews**, dating from the 1890s, has gone up-market into housing and offices.

The genteel and vaguely rural name of **MAYGROVE ROAD** was approved in 1869. It formerly comprised Sampford Terrace, Maygrove Villas, Cheltenham Villas, Bankside and Rockfield Terrace. Most of the houses on the south side are in Middlesex stock brick and, from their red brick decoration and other stylistic differences, it can be seen how they were built in groups. But the overall decorative standard is surprisingly high. Note also the ironwork on **Nos. 2–4**. A number of houses have kept their original front railings and their names: **Nos. 28–30, 40, 48, 54** are labelled Langport, Hanover, Holly, York and Teviot House and **Nos. 58–60** are Maygrove Villas. Decorative detail is particularly good on **Nos. 28–34** and **46–54**. Two stained glass artists, F.W. Noble and J.B. Payne, were working at **No. 48** and **No. 58** respectively in 1885: Noble stayed on until *c*1938. **No. 64**, Acacia Villa, was a ladies school in the 1880s. The semi-detached houses **Nos. 98–100** and **102–104** bear the initials JEM, perhaps those of the builder just mentioned, John Edward Medley. On the north side of the road, **Nos. 55–57** are on the site of St Cuthbert's Mission Hall, built in 1894. The flats over the shops are called **Lauriston**, possibly after Lauriston Lodge (*q.v.*). Next to the Mission Hall were the depots of the Anglo-American Oil Company and the General (later British) Petroleum Company, both of whom departed in the early 1930s. This stretch of the road is still in industrial use. The garage at **No. 59** was for over half a century Maygrove Motors – 'one of Camden's oldest established firms' says the inscription (inaccurately) on the garage wall. The 1987 mural happily celebrates the West End Sidings Estate, which heads north from here (and is dealt with below). **No. 65**, Handrail House, owes its name to F.J. Lewis, who started as a wooden handrail maker at 3 Blackburn Road in 1922, moved south to Exeter Mews in 1928 and west to his present site in 1936. Here he built a factory, mainly of timber, and in 1950 the present building (extended 1960), which the Lewis family firm still partly occupies. The strikingly idiosyncratic **No. 67**, suitably housing a computer bureau, has recently replaced Charles Mordell House on this site. In the early 1980s the adjoining land was turned into

Maygrove Peace Park, landscaped on several levels and including play areas for children. Set into the paths are stone slabs engraved with quotations from peace-loving notables such as Albert Einstein and John Lennon. Outside the Sidings Community Centre (see below) is a bronze **statue** by Anthony Gormley said to be 'a listening figure'. At the east end of Maygrove Road, **No. 73** (once Ariel Works) used to produce buttons but now manufactures laboratory and clinical supplies. Across the road, **Nos. 164–170** are particularly rich in decorative detail. **No. 140's** archway leads to an extensive yard which in Edwardian times included a zinc-working factory. Another yard behind **No. 128** houses the thriving Done-Our-Bit Club, which began as an ex-servicemen's club in Kilburn High Road (now a Pizza Hut) and moved here about 1925. The premises were enlarged in 1930 (architect: Percival Ware) to include a stage and a hall to seat 300. A plaque commemorates the opening of the Maygrove (Remembrance) Hall by Major General Lord Loch.

To the north of Maygrove Road is the **West End Sidings Estate**, bounded by Fordwych Road and the old Midland Railway. In the early 1970s the disused railway sidings had become a derelict overgrown area of almost sixteen acres, earmarked for use by Ringway One, the Inner London Motorway Scheme. When the GLC scrapped the motorway proposals in 1974, Camden drew up plans for housing some 300 families on this site, together with old people's housing, a hostel for young people, an open space, sports hall, allotments and a community centre. Building began after three years of fierce local debate and most of the plans were carried out. The housing enclave consists of **BARLOW ROAD** leading to **BRASSEY ROAD** and the pedestrian **HALL OAK WALK**. The first two names derive from the adjoining railway line. Thomas Brassey was the contractor responsible for the line's construction and W.H. Barlow designed St Pancras train shed. Hall Oak was the name of the manor farm. The lively **Sidings Community Centre** at No. 150 Brassey Road includes the Apostolic Church of God. To the east, the cul-de-sac **LIDDELL ROAD** (named after a local estate) was built in 1984 to accommodate small industries and workshops. The estate is linked to Mill Lane by **Wayne Kirkum Way** (*q.v.*).

17. The remains of *Kilburn Priory* in 1722.

Up Kilburn High Road

The early history of Kilburn is chiefly the story of Kilburn Priory. It stood on the Roman Watling Street, roughly where the present Belsize Road meets Kilburn High Road, but its last traces disappeared in the early nineteenth century. Park includes in his *Topography* the copy of an etching of the only piece left standing in 1722. According to the *Victoria County History*, the name Kilburn derived from Cuneburna, first noted *c*1134, meaning royal or possibly cow's stream: others have held it to mean 'cold water', descriptive of the stream that ran through the area.

Some time in the twelfth century a hermit called Godwyn who lived on the banks of this stream, gave his cell into the hands of Abbot Herbert of Westminster, who founded there a nunnery, of which Godwyn was appointed master and warden for life. The first three nuns were Emma, Gunhilda and Christina, supposedly maids of honour to Henry I's queen, Matilda. In the Middle Ages the forests in this area were almost impenetrable and infested by outlaws and beasts of prey. Deforestation began in 1218 and by the fourteenth century the road was safe enough to become the chief pilgrim route to St Albans. This traffic eventually became such a burden to the nuns that additional revenue had to be provided by the Abbot of Westminster. At the Dissolution of the Monasteries Henry

VIII exchanged the Priory with the Knights of St John of Jerusalem for their manor of Paris Garden, Southwark. Four years later, however, it was again seized by the king and passed into a succession of lay hands. In 1850, on widening the railway, various small articles and some old foundations were discovered. Also found later was an ancient brass, still preserved in St Mary's Church, Abbey Road (*q.v.*).

Cruchley's map of 1829 gives the best picture of **KILBURN HIGH ROAD** in early times. Its principal buildings are clustered round the straight line of Watling Street (later Edgware Road) and to the south, beyond the present borough boundary, is **Pine Apple Place**, where George Romney had lodgings in 1793. At the end of Greville Place, a section of the High Road was called Kilburn Priory – a name since reallocated – and here was a toll-gate at which vehicles were charged one penny a wheel. It was removed to Willesden Lane in 1864. (A tall block on the west side of the road is now called Tollgate House.) At this point of the High Road, there used to be a bridge over the river Kilburn. The river had meandered southwards through the Kilburn meadows, where Keats first recited his *Ode to a Nightingale* to his friend, the artist Benjamin Haydon, who wrote that the poet spoke 'in a low tremulous undertone

which affected me greatly'.

Concentrating on the Hampstead side of the High Road (the west side is in Brent) the southern stretch begins with **Nos. 1–6 The Parade**, developed from a florist-cum-nursery in 1900. Seven years later at **Nos. 9–11** arrived the New Empire Theatre of Varieties, as a music hall and circus. It was an ornate, three-storey building, which seated nearly two thousand and had a stage equipped with animal traps and pits. These survived its conversion into The Kilburn Empire in 1928, which became a cinema, called the Essoldo, about 1950, later The Broadway and, after much alteration, The Classic in 1971. By then the building was clad in sheet metal. Now it is clad in hoarding and boarding. Further entertainment was offered nearby at **No. 4 Kilburn High Road**, the Kilburn Conservatoire in the 1890s, and at **No. 10**, the Kilburn Electric Palace in the 1910s. (From here, note the old houses behind the shops of Nos. 6–8.)

The Red Lion has a handsome plaster lion and a plaque recording its establishment in 1444, no doubt then due to its proximity to the Priory; its latest rebuilding was in 1890. Decorations include two handsome lamp brackets. Next door, **Nos. 34a–36a**, plastered with initials and other frills, were opened in 1884 as William Roper's Drapery Emporium. (The date and initials can be seen round the corner in Springfield Lane.) By 1896 this had become part of Kilburn Bon Marché (see below). Next door is **The Old Bell** (sometimes Ye Olde Bell and in the 1899 Directory confusingly Ye Olde Belle) dated as a building back to 1863, and as an

18. *Toll gate* at the south end of Kilburn High Road, corner of Kilburn Priory, 1860.

19. *The Bell Inn*, Kilburn Wells, 1797.

institution back to about 1600. Both this pub and the Red Lion are presumed (by the *Victoria County History*) to stand on the site of a mansion and a *hostium* attached to Kilburn Priory. By 1714 a medicinal well was being exploited nearby and the area was dignified by the title Kilburn Wells. A Great Room was advertised as being particularly adapted for 'the amusement of the politest companies' and the Old Bell charged threepence a glass for chalybeate water. The pleasures of the area were promoted in *Stanzas on Kilburn Wells and its Situation* by T.S., which began

Where sweet sequester'd scenes inspire delight,
And simple Nature joins with ev'ry art,
At KILBURN WELLS their various charms unite,
And gladly all conspire to please the heart.

20. *Kilburn High Road*, corner of Belsize Road, in late Victorian times.

As late as 1821, a poster announced performances at the New Theatre, Kilburn Wells, adding 'Roads well watched and lighted'. The Tea Gardens in the grounds, opened by 1733, attracted thousands of visitors and it was from here that the last traces of the Priory could be seen until about 1840, when the railway had arrived.

On the site of **No. 40** was built in 1884 another outpost of Roper's Drapery empire, later known as Kilburn Bon Marché. There were further depots in Osborne Terrace and Goldsmith Place but by 1932 the empire had crumbled and the London Cooperative Society had moved in.

Local residents were petitioning for a **railway station** in this area as early as 1846 and got it five years later, but the original entrance to the LNWR platforms was in Belsize Road (*q.v.*). About a century ago, it was called Kilburn and Maida Vale Station and a part of the old incised name-plaque can still be seen at the corner with Belsize Road. Across this road, the bank building at **No. 42**, which also held a bank in the 1880s, bears a plaque claiming 'This was the site of Kilburn Wells'. From the turn of the last century (until the 1970s), the important local architect G.A. Sexton (later 'and Sons') was also based here. (A thesis on his work is in the Local Studies Library.) Specialising in commercial architecture, Sexton converted **Nos. 50–56** into another large drapery shop, David Fearn & Co., but this was partly replaced by British Home Stores in 1930. The pleasant facade includes the date. No. 50 was also the home (by 1899) of the Kilburn Athenaeum, used for concerts, dancing lessons and, in 1905, for 'the Pierrot Troupe's comic medleys', reported by the *Kilburn Times*. Marks & Spencer, who opened at **Nos. 66–8** about 1930, had started with a Penny Bazaar on the other side of the High Road in 1907. Their present imposing frontage has classical columns of what can only be called a composite order. Next door, **No. 70** has four intriguing circular medallions on its walls, containing assorted male heads. They are thought to be famous musicians, as these premises were occupied from the 1890s to at least 1930 by Alfred Phillips Ltd, pianoforte dealers. Note the united front of **Nos. 86–98** with windows flanked by columns and topped by decorative tiles. See also on No. 86 the antique burglar alarm called 'Rely-a-Bell'. In the 1890s **No. 128** was occupied by

21. The fire at B.B. Evans, 1910.

Sainsbury's, who with Lilley & Skinner (then at Nos. 260–2) were among the earliest multiple stores to establish local outlets.

And so to B.B. Evans. **Nos. 142–162** once constituted the High Road's famous department store, started by Benjamin Beardmore Evans in 1897 as a draper's. (Why did Kilburn need so much drapery?) In 1905, G.A. Sexton (see above) was commissioned to turn eight adjoining premises into one vast store. Despite a terrible fire in 1910, B.B. Evans grew into an important local landmark and many

West Hampstead residents will remember buying their school uniforms there. In 1962, when it changed hands, the store was employing five hundred people: but in 1971, described as 'Kilburn's only department store', it closed down.

The Coopers Arms was for many years a beer shop run by the Titmuss family, but was promoted to a pub by 1930. A Titmuss was still in charge in 1970. The pub-sign properly shows the cooper's trade. At the corner with Gascony Avenue, **No. 218** still has Pritchard's carved in stone on its windows: this was a restaurant and baker's shop in the 1920s and '30s. **No. 228** has a fancy ironwork notice, offering cash loans, jewellery and diamonds. As the three-ball sign suggests, there were pawnbrokers here – in the 1880s, George Arnold and, in the 1980s, as mentioned in the notice, G.W. and A.E. Thomson. In this stretch of the High Road once stood Clarence House, where the young Thomas Hardy lodged in 1861–2. He was at this time assistant to the architect (Sir) Arthur Blomfield, whom Hardy helped to supervise the evacuation of graves when the Midland Railway cut through Old St Pancras Churchyard. Round the corner of **No. 232** (in Messina Avenue) an old advertisement, painted on the wall, exhorts you to 'Buy Gillette'.

Between **Nos. 234–6** was the frontage of Kilburn's stateliest home, The Grange, which first appears in the Rate Books of 1833. The house was built by Samuel Ware, architect to the Duke of Portland, who had in 1831 previously built (a little to the south) another respectable residence, Oak Lodge, (see Kingsgate Road). The two properties covered much of the old Little Estate, which appeared in the 1762 Estate Map as John Bowden's farm. From 1843 The Grange was occupied by the family of Thomas Peters (c1786–1863), a wealthy coach builder, with workshops and showrooms near Marble Arch: Queen Victoria was among his clients. Ada, his daughter-in-law, remained in the house, Kilburn's last mansion, until 1910. Known locally as 'Lady Peters', she was occasionally seen riding in her carriage down the High Road with a footman dressed in chocolate-coloured livery. After her death the contents of The Grange were quickly auctioned and included four coaches, a horse-drawn lawnmower and a Merryweather fire engine. Efforts to preserve the house failed but 8½ acres of the grounds were purchased in 1911 by the councils of Hampstead and Willesden and the county councils of London and Middlesex: the price was £19,500, of which £600 was raised by public subscription. Together with five acres of an old market garden, the result was **Kilburn Grange Park**, still a popular open space, approached from the High Road by **GRANGEWAY**. Some of The Grange's high garden wall, topped with urns(?) can still be seen in the park.

Among those who wanted to develop the High Road frontage of the estate was Sir Oswald Stoll, who planned a Kilburn Coliseum on the same lines as his Coliseum in St Martin's Lane. Hampstead Council successfully opposed this, backed by schools in Kingsgate Road and Netherwood Street who petitioned that 'the attendance of young people at places of entertainment 3 or 4 times a week could not fit them for the work they would have to do in life'. A smaller-scale distraction did, however, materialise on this site in 1911 in the shape of The Biograph Theatre but this was superseded in 1914 by the famous Grange Cinema. The name can still be seen in plasterwork on this Listed Building, which has since 1976 been occupied by a night club, the **National Club**. The cinema was designed by Edward Stone, architect of many other super-cinemas, and

22. *The Grange*, on Kilburn High Road.

with over 2,000 seats was one of the largest in Europe. The grand organ and the Winter Garden Café have gone but much of the ornate interior decor has survived. Note the stained glass windows at first floor level!

Higher up the High Road, the **Sir Colin Campbell** pub has been operating only since the early 1950s: it is presumably named after the suppressor of the Indian Mutiny (1858), a surprising choice. Nearby, an older rival, the **Black Lion**, dates back to 1666, but it was 'Rebuilt 1898', as the decorative sign says. The style is Flemish Gothic, according to the DoE which Listed the building. The turret-ted corner windows are particularly attractive. Another tavern at the corner of Palmerston Road, **The Roman Way**, was in existence by 1880 as the Palmerston Hotel. This later became the Lord Palmerston public house, which closed in 1977. The present title is presumably celebrating the pub's location on the old Roman Watling Street.

No. 318 bears the date 1901 and **Nos. 320–22** show (at the top) part of their old name 'Alexanders' Stores'. Specialising in ironmongery, china and glass, the firm was there from at least 1896. **No. 336** also displays its date 1881; about which time it was a dairy. On the other side of Iverson Road, **Spring Court**, a block of sheltered flats for the elderly, was built by 1990 on the site of the Brondesbury Baptist Church. This striking building, seating 780, stood here from 1878 but was closed in 1980 to make way for the flats and a new smaller church (see Iverson Road).

The High Road is here crossed by three railway **bridges** belonging to the Chiltern Line and the Underground (Jubilee and Metropolitan Lines). One is inscribed 'Metropolitan Railway 1914'. An enormous engineering operation was mounted in 1977 to replace the upper bridges, the last cast-iron bridges on the Underground, with a new steel deck.

Kilburn High Road is now a lively and successful shopping centre. Business began in earnest in about 1870, according to the *Wembley History Society* (see *Journal* in Local Studies Library) and by 1909 there were over 300 shops, including over 40 drapery and allied trades. Building spread from south to north and there are, according to the *Victoria County History*, 'examples from every decade from the 1860s…The earlier stucco and stock brick gave way to the red brick terraced and semi-detached houses of the northern Powell-Cotton estate'. Today, the shops, pubs and small factories are also of great variety and reflect 'the successive waves of immigrants that have given Kilburn its cosmopolitan flavour'.

The north-western corner of this sector has been developed twice in a century and is now dominated by an extensive complex of buildings rejoicing in the Worcestershire name of **Webheath**. This council estate has largely replaced the original development of the area by the United Land Company in 1869, when directors of the company apparently gave their names to **NETHERWOOD STREET** and **LINSTEAD STREET**. They also built a Kelson Street here but this has been wiped out by Webheath. Charles Kelson was a retired East India merchant and a shareholder of the company. Netherwood Street was originally called Royston Road after a nearby house called Royston Hall (*q.v.*). Several social services were available in the street in the 1890s including a dispensary for the poor, a Girls' Help Society and a Working Men's Gospel Temperance Mission. Despite all this welfare, the heavily overpopulated street was declared in 1910 to be the unhealthiest part of the borough. Today, there are few buildings left. The most unusual is the council's new **Netherwood Day Centre**, opened (by Dr Jonathan Miller) in 1990 for dementia sufferers: the exterior design by David Kerley is vaguely Egyptian. The garden features a shelter in the form of a pagoda. Perhaps inspired by the street's name, the council has recently started a new **wood** here, next to the North London railway. A derelict area designed for allotments, but little used except by travellers, has been planted with two hundred trees, together with bulbs and woodland flowers. At the far end of the road is the vast old Board School, now the Lower School of **St George's Catholic Comprehensive**. This was built in 1881 to hold 300 boys,

300 girls and 400 infants, and was notable for its evening classes and cookery centre. High on the building, along with the usual floral terracotta, can be seen plaques saying 'School Board for London' and 'Netherwood Street School 1881'. It was later known as Harben Senior School and its address was Kelson Street. The entrance is now in Linstead Street.

PALMERSTON ROAD was built (by Donald Nicoll) in 1865, soon after Lord Palmerston's death. The Wells and Campden Charity erected its first set of baths and wash-houses here in 1887 but they had to be closed in 1976 by the council, then the owners, on economic grounds. Their demolition was accelerated by an explosion in the building, which blew out some two hundred windows on the Webheath Estate and badly damaged the annexe to St George's R.C. Comprehensive School. The middle section of Palmerston Road has been taken over by Webheath and here is the **foundation stone** for the estate, laid in 1968 by the Mayor of Camden. The estate was opened by the council in two stages, in 1970 and 1972, following the biggest compulsory purchase order in its history. Housing on various levels was designed by the borough architect, Sidney Cook, to accommodate four hundred people and to exclude tower blocks. The community centre here is called **Cayford Hall** after Dame Florence Cayford, a leading light of the Hampstead Labour Party and once dubbed 'the uncrowned queen of Kilburn'.

POWELL-COTTONS AGAIN

The history of the Powell-Cotton Estate has been given in the previous section of this book, which described the property of Shoot-up Hill. The family also owned an estate on both sides of West End Lane and, as before, most of the streets here derive their names from places in north-east Kent, near the family seat at Quex Park, Birchington. (The house and the adjoining Powell-Cotton Museum are frequently open to the public.) This seat was once owned by a family called Quekes, which explains the name.

QUEX ROAD was the first to be laid out, dating back to 1866. In an estate map of 1871 the road is given the name of Abbey Road West, but it is unlikely that this was ever official. The first impression of Quex Road is of entering an ecclesiastical stronghold. The short road is dominated by the Roman Catholic **Church of the Sacred Heart of Jesus**. The Oblates of Mary Immaculate came to London in 1865, stepped off the bus at the Cock Tavern in Kilburn High Road and chose the site amid green fields. A temporary church was built in 1868 and the distinguished architect E.W. Pugin (son of the more famous A.W. Pugin) was commissioned to prepare plans for a permanent church, which was finally opened by Cardinal Manning in 1879. First called New Priory, this church stood until 1962, when the present extensive buildings were designed by F.G.

Broadbent. **No. 14** Quex Road, home of the Arendzen family, four of whom were priests, was bought by the church and turned into an employment agency and headquarters of the Legion of Mary. **Hope House**, opposite the church, was established by the Holy Family Sisters as a nursing home in 1876. This has now been incorporated with the house next door and a newly-built extension at the back and a rebuilt house on the west side, all called **Conway House**, providing a hostel for Irish youths. To remind them of home, a green Irish 'telefon' kiosk stands in the grounds. **No. 22** was the home for some years of a well-known Victorian stained glass artist, Nathaniel Westlake, some of whose work is in St James's, Sherriff Road.

On the west side of the Catholic church is the **Wesleyan Methodist Church**, opened in 1963 on the site of the original chapel of 1869. The adjoining **Church Hall** has four foundation stones dated 1905. The architects were Bell, Withers and Meredith. On the east side is the **Unitarian Church**, built in 1896 and closed down in 1965, when its congregation had dwindled to five. At present, it is being used by the Catholic church as a soup kitchen. Among the few houses on the north side of the road, **Nos. 8–15** offer fanciful facades. At the end of 1991 **St Mary's Primary School** (Church of England) moved up from the bottom of

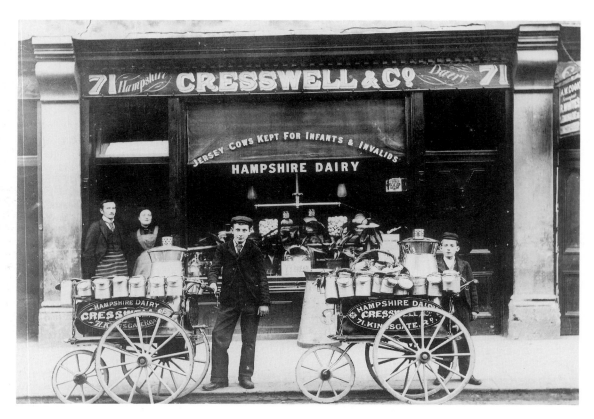

23. *Cresswell's Dairy*, 71 Kingsgate Road, *c*1895.

West End Lane (*q.v.*) to the corner of Quex Road: the architect was Hans Haenlein. **Douglas Court** (1896) and **King's Gardens** (1897) occupy the site of The Chimes (*q.v.*). Until 1988 **QUEX MEWS** contained old stables and a wall-sign offering 'Broughams, Landaus or Victorias for any period' from the firm of J. Ives and Sons Ltd. The Mews now has newly-built town houses and apartments but has kept the cobbled approach. Another cobbled offshoot, **LEITH YARD**, gives access to the rear of shops on Kilburn High Road.

To the south, **BIRCHINGTON ROAD** was laid out and fully built up by 1880. The houses are remarkable only for the original stained glass and the iron strapwork on their front doors. The eastern stretch of the road has developed into **BRANSDALE CLOSE**, a cul-de-sac on the newer portion of the Kilburn Vale Estate: this includes the pleasant **Sycamore Court**. The name of **MUTRIX ROAD**, approved in 1866, came from one of the farms on the Powell-Cotton Estate in Margate, which belonged to one Alfred Motryk, *c*1250. By 1885 the only building in the road was St Dominic's School, which by the 1920s became St Mary's Men's Club. In 1965 there were no residents at all in Mutrix Road but by 1980 it had become part of the Council's **Kilburn Vale Estate**. To judge by the new front doors and coach lamps, almost all of these houses are now in private hands, resulting from the Government's 'Right to Buy' scheme.

To the north, **MAZENOD AVENUE**, formerly called Plazley Road, was named after Charles de Mazenod (1782–1861), Bishop of Marseilles: he was founder of the Oblate Fathers, who built the Church of the Sacred Heart in Quex Road. On the east side is the **Mazenod RC Primary School** and the **New Mazenod Social Centre** with a foundation stone laid by the mayor, Patrick O'Connor, in 1966. **New**

Priory Court has been built on the site of a multi-style mansion block called Priory Court. The houses opposite are particularly rich in fruity and foliar stonework. Note also the Edwardian **postbox**.

KINGSGATE ROAD has another East Kent place-name, though there is the usual local legend that here was the gateway to King Henry VIII's hunting estates. The Oak Lodge Estate map of about 1875 shows Kingsgate Road built as far north as Smyrna Road: the Oak Lodge grounds stretched from the High Road right back as far as West End Lane, blocking any further development. The house had been built by Samuel Ware in 1831 and one of its last owners was Frederick James Clark, land agent for the Maryon Wilson estate: he was also a partner in Farebrother, Clark and Lye, among the biggest estate agents in London. Oak Lodge was sold in 1879 and within two years building had begun on Messina and Gascony Avenues. On the west of Kingsgate Road now is the Council's **Kingsgate Estate**.

ERESBY PLACE is a remnant of Eresby Road, built about 1880, and perhaps named after a place in Lincolnshire. The other estate roads are **GRANGE PLACE** (after Kilburn Grange), **QUEENSGATE PLACE** (presumably to match Kingsgate and to show Camden's Equal Opportunities policy) and **FIRE ENGINE ROAD** (self-evident?). Among those occupying a short-life, housing association flat in Kingsgate Road in the 1980s was Ken Livingstone, the last leader of the Greater London Council. The mostly cobbled **KINGSGATE PLACE** once housed builders and sawmills but notably the stables for over 200 horses of the London General Omnibus Company. Now it has one old cottage and some new industrial units. Painted on the wall at the junction with Kingsgate Road can still be seen the names of the road's occupants in the 1930s – Rumbold's, 'aircraft upholsterers', Harris, engineers, and the garage of B.B. Evans Department Store.

SMYRNA ROAD followed the boundary of a large field on the Oak Lodge Estate, thus accounting for the sharp right-angle bend in the road. Here, in an otherwise ordinary road, **Smyrna Mansions** rises impressively. The names of this road and of **MESSINA AVENUE** and **GASCONY AVENUE** have not been explained but may commemorate a Powell-Cotton Grand Tour. Many of the houses here were being demolished in the 1970s but others were reprieved and refurbished. Most have well-ornamented frontages, notably **Nos. 87–9** Messina Avenue with a riot of bird life and foliage. **No. 56** has a plaque with initials and date – HS 1883. **Nos 56–68** were originally called Richmond Villas.

Returning to Kingsgate Road, it is a joy to find so many small shops which give a village-like atmosphere to this crowded part of London. At the corner with Messina Avenue, the handsomely turreted **Kingsgate Primary School** bears its date (1903) and the initials of the London School Board. One of its archways is labelled 'Special School Boys'. To the north is one of the oldest buildings in the road, which originated as Barnes' Furniture Repository. Reopened in 1978 as the **Kingsgate Workshops** and surviving threats of demolition, the building now houses over 60 different craftsmen and women working in light industry and art studios. Opposite, the Council's **Health and Welfare Centre** was the dream-come-true of Hampstead's remarkable pioneer of social services, Thomas Hancock Nunn. His name is little known now, except on a block of flats in Fellows Road, but a portrait plaque here records his fight to unite all the social services under one roof. Foundation stones note that his Hampstead Health Institute was opened in 1913 by Princess Louise and enlarged in 1929. St George's Hall, now the **Kingsgate Community Centre**, was opened by Mrs Stanley Baldwin on St George's Day 1929. By the time Nunn died in 1937, it was widely recognised as 'an instrument of health, knowledge, recreation and righteousness'. The present Community Centre has a lively programme with an international flavour, with groups of local Irish, Somalis and Asians and a café with Latin American chefs.

In 1878 the Oaklands Hall Estate, on the site of **DYNHAM ROAD** and **COTLEIGH ROAD**, was built over the grounds of Oaklands Hall (see West End Lane). Dynham Road still has most of its original houses and those towards the foot of the hill are notably well-kept. The only building of note in Cotleigh Road is the **Library**, the first purpose-built branch library in Hampstead, dated 1901. The names of these two roads were officially approved in 1882 but the derivation is obscure. (Cotleigh is a place in South Devon.)

By the 1870s the West End Lane section of the Powell-Cotton Estate was ripe for development and Colonel Cotton envisaged a better class of property here'. Between 1877 and 1886 large well-spaced houses were built in **ACOL ROAD**, **WOODCHURCH ROAD** and **CLEVE ROAD**, all with East Kent place-names. Acol Road was laid out and built between 1877–79. In the early 1930s **No. 15** housed the Acol Bridge Club, now in West End Lane, some of whose members originated the system of bidding which still bears this name. St John Philby, diplomat, traveller, and champion of Arab nationalism, kept **No. 18** as a home for his wife and children. His son, the double agent Kim Philby, is now probably better known. **Acol Court** was built in 1934 on the site of a large house in West End Lane called Queen's Lodge. Doris Bailey, Hampstead's second woman mayor (1955–57), lived at 40 Acol Court: she served on Hampstead Borough Council from 1945–1964. Note the Victorian **postbox** at the corner with Priory Road.

Woodchurch Road was named in 1882, but building began in 1878–79 and the date 1880 can be seen on **No. 8**. The artist Seymour Lucas (1849–1923) had a studio at **No. 1** (New Place) from 1882 to 1904 and somewhat incongruously imported a Queen Anne doorway from Fairfax House, Putney. This still welcomes visitors to the house, which was also said to contain a Tudor fireplace, some Jacobean panelling and doors dating from 1637. Note the dragons on the roofs of **Nos. 3** and **5**. On the north side, **Olive and Douglas Waite Houses** have a nicely complex, hexagonal arrangement. The flats, **Aran Lodge**, were built in 1985 to designs by Martin Beaton Associates. **Nos. 12–14** are an ornate Gothic pair with good bargeboards. On the site of **Sidney Boyd Court** (see West End Lane) was Anglebay, the home of the distinguished architect, Banister Fletcher senior (1833–99). Apart from owning and designing local property (see Compayne Gardens) he was a revered Professor of Architecture at King's College, London, and the author, with his son, the more famous Sir Banister Flight Fletcher, of the first edition of the monumental *History of Architecture on the Comparative Method*. He was also a JP, MP

for NW Wiltshire and Master of the Worshipful Company of Carpenters. Much of this can be gleaned from his handsome tombstone in Hampstead Cemetery.

Cleve Road was built in 1882–86. Much has since been rebuilt but the name Woodcote, shown in the 1885–6 Directory, can still be seen on the gate of the near-derelict **No. 16**. Charles Stuart, an artist who exhibited at the Royal Academy from 1896–1902, lived at **No. 1** (The Hermitage). The flats at **Cleve House** were built in 1935 and those at **Embassy House** in 1936–37. The Paul Balint-AJR Day Centre at **No. 15** opened in 1987 and provides a wide range of activities and entertainments for members of the Association of Jewish Refugees. Note the old coach house at **No. 19** with antlers on top. **No. 21** (Jackson House), a project of the West Hampstead Housing Cooperative, was opened in 1990 by the actress and, later, the Member of Parliament for Hampstead and Highgate, Glenda Jackson.

Between Acol Road and Priory Road, **WAVEL MEWS**, named in 1879 after Thomas Bruce Wavel, a local landowner, provided ten stables for the southern part of the estate. Taylor's Stores, a business begun here in 1929 and closed in 1978, offered a real amenity for the area. All of the stables have now been converted to residences and several new houses were built in the 1960s and 1970s, but the old cobbles have remained.

24. Part of Cruchley's folding map of 1829, with the new Finchley Road sketched in.

THE ABBEY FARM ESTATE

In the south-west corner of the borough, the Abbey Farm Estate occupied the site of Kilburn Priory (*q.v.*) and its surrounding lands.

At the Dissolution of the Monasteries this land was granted to Robert, Earl of Sussex, and in 1546 was given by the Crown to John, Earl of Warwick. The estate subsequently passed through many private hands until it was purchased in 1819 by Fulke Greville Howard, whose wife, Mary Howard, owned large estates in various parts of the country. Howard was born an Upton but, influenced perhaps by Mary's great wealth, he took his wife's name on their marriage.

Howard had bought Abbey Farm as a speculation and he started its development in 1820. Various difficulties were encountered, however, and by 1825 only half a dozen large villas in the Greville Place area had been built. George Pocock, an Islington builder, who was chosen to start this project, fell victim to the commercial panic in the City in 1825, when over 700 banks closed owing to the activities of bubble companies. George Pocock lived at No. 2 Kilburn Priory and later lived and died at No. 7 Kilburn Priory, now **136 Maida Vale**. Part of this house (in a near derelict condition) survives and bears a **blue plaque** to William Friese-Greene (1855–1921), the pioneer of cinematography.

George Pocock left his name on a public house in the Caledonian Road. For more about the Pococks and the Greville Estate see *The Diary of a London Schoolboy* by John Thomas Pocock, edited by Marjorie Holder and Christina Gee (Camden History Society, 1980).

At **No. 140 Maida Vale**, just inside the borough boundary, are the grandiose Carlton Rooms, as early as 1914 a cinema, called the Maida Vale Palace. They became a Mecca Social Club in 1961, which means bingo seven days a week, and are reputed to be the first commercial bingo hall in the country: the domed roof with its rich plaster work is worth a look inside.

In the nineteenth century, the southern sector of this estate was in the borough of St Marylebone. This may explain why **GREVILLE PLACE**, now on the boundary between the London Borough of Camden and the City of Westminster, has a touch of St John's Wood about it. There is here and in adjoining roads an air of peace and spaciousness and, although the houses are of differing styles of architecture, they blend in well with one another. Several of the early nineteenth century houses have survived and **Nos. 1–5** are Listed Buildings.

No. 1 (with a fine fanlight) was once occupied by the Duke of Atholl and **No. 3** (the unhappy looking Greville

25. *Sir Frank Dicksee* of Greville Place, sculpted by Sir Goscombe John of Greville Road, 1907.

House) by Sir Frank Dicksee (1853–1928), President of the Royal Academy at the time of his death here. The Greville Place **Nature Reserve**, set up in 1985 at the rear of No. 1, includes a wayfaring tree planted in 1990 in memory of Keith Valdar, a worker at the London Wildlife Reserve. John Hutton (1907–1978), the artist and glass engraver, lived at **No. 3A** during 1966–75. He designed the Great Glass Screen in Coventry Cathedral, which took him ten years to complete. **Nos. 13–19** are also on the DoE List as mid-nineteenth century buildings of Italianate design. Nos. 13–15 have attractive shell decoration. **Ascot Lodge**, which was built in 1939, has recently been vigorously refurbished.

A backwater from Greville Place, **BOLTON ROAD**, was named after a local land-lessee, Henry Bolton. It used to link up with Alexandra Road, but the Abbey Estate has cut it short and altogether wiped out its tributary, Holtham Road. **Nos. 2–8** Bolton Road (with a long handsome balcony) housed an artists' colony in the 1870s and later No. 4 was converted to the St Augustine's Mission Rooms.

GREVILLE ROAD, also named after Fulke Greville Howard, was laid out by his nephew and heir, Colonel Arthur Upton. Potter's map of 1820 shows it as a footpath but on the Lucas map of 1845 the southern part is being developed and called Carlton Place. By 1854 more groups of villas had appeared and the present name is shown on the 1866 OS map. Among the sturdy late-Victorian villas are a few delightful earlier houses, especially the Listed Buildings **Nos. 24, 25** and **26A** which were formerly one residence. Behind the enormous arched window at first floor level is a studio where the prolific sculptor Sir William Goscombe John (1860–1952) worked from 1892 until his death. His bronze statues are to be found all over the world, from Eastbourne to Baghdad, round Westminster Abbey, St Paul's and the Horse Guards Parade: his George V and Queen Mary dominate the Mersey Tunnel. He was knighted immediately after an earlier royal assignment, designing the regalia for the Prince of Wales's Investiture at Caernarvon Castle in 1911; he is buried in Hampstead Cemetery (q.v.). Opposite, **No. 35** and Regency Lodge, **No. 37**, with the lions' heads at the gate, are attractive mid-Victorian houses, but only the latter is on the DoE List. From 1938 until he was bombed out in 1940, the visionary artist Albert Houthuesen (b. 1903) lived there. Even the **mews** alongside No. 37, although quite modern, has acquired a kind of olde-worlde charm. Continuing the artistic tradition, Willi Soukop RA, noted for his wood sculpture, now lives in this road.

KILBURN PRIORY is somewhat confusing. At the time Howard began his development, the name was applied to houses in the Edgware Road (Maida Vale) on either side of Greville Place, and on Cruchley's map of 1835 the present Kilburn Priory is marked simply as Private Road. On the 1866 OS map it is shown as an extension of Priory Road but by 1873 it had received its present name. There is little in the road now to remind us of the nineteenth century but a modern block of flats named **Goldsmith's Place**, perpetuating the vanished name of a nearby street (see below) and the memory of the great Oliver Goldsmith who once lived there.

On the west side of Kilburn Priory is a pocket of small streets dating from the mid-nineteenth century; the original houses being built by James Carter (1845–49) and George Duncan (1851–57). The name-changers have had a great time here: Goldsmith Place, Osborne Terrace and Bell Terrace are merged into **SPRINGFIELD LANE**; Manchester Mews (1865–1934) is changed to **GREVILLE MEWS**;

Springfield Gardens and Manchester Terrace have become **SPRINGFIELD WALK**, and Springfield Road, once joining Greville Road to Kilburn High Road, is now just a westward extension of Greville Road. As one might guess, there was once a spring in a field hereabouts, near the junction of Kilburn High Road and Belsize Road. Next to **No. 36A** Springfield Lane is a curious blocked doorway and the initials and date, WR 1884. These doubtless refer to William Roper, who had a large drapery business in this area. Greville Mews still has three of its original coach houses and most of this backwater is still devoted to transport though 'baker' can be read on **No. 20**. The only house of note in Springfield Walk is at the junction with Kilburn Priory: **No. 11** is on the 1894 OS map. In Springfield Lane there is an intriguing back entrance to the **Red Lion** and a nearly obscured advertisement for the London Co-op. **Nos. 6–12** recall a pretty cottage development very different from George Pocock's mansions in Greville Place.

MORTIMER PLACE and **MORTIMER CRESCENT** were named after Thomas Hill Mortimer of Albany, Piccadilly, who was Colonel Upton's agent when he laid out these roads from 1853–60. Some of the old trees have happily survived but the original houses are fast disappearing. **Hillsborough Court** is a semi-mock-Tudor block of flats of 1934 with some stone heraldry without and an unusual cloistered layout within. **Broadoak** and **Haliwell Houses** (1955) are on the site of St Peter's Convent and Henley House School, a boys' school, boasting A.A. Milne's father as Headmaster, H.G. Wells as a science teacher and Alfred Harmsworth as a pupil. Christopher Robin's father was born here in 1882. Nearby was North Hall, bombed during World War II, the home of the poet, John Drinkwater, from 1934 until his death in 1937. **Nos. 6**

and **7**, and **17** and **18** Mortimer Crescent are the only original houses still standing. Charles Douglas-Home (1937–1986), editor of *The Times*, lived at No. 18 and George Orwell (1903–1950) was at **No. 10** in 1943–4.

At the northern end of Mortimer Crescent, part of the old Alexandra Road (*q.v.*) has been chopped off by the new housing estate and given the name of **LANGTRY ROAD**. It was intended that it should be called Gunhilda Road, in memory of one of the nuns who founded Kilburn Priory, but a breath of scandal proved more attractive than the odour of sanctity (or royalty), and it has been subsequently named after Alexandra Road's notorious resident, the 'Jersey Lily'. **Nos. 1–6** are the only survivals from the 1860s, when the road was built: No. 1, which looks like a studio, was a school at the turn of the century.

The rest of the Abbey Farm Estate, between West End Lane and the old London North Western Railway, is close to the site of the old Kilburn Priory. The earliest road in this area was the Kilburn High Road end of **BELSIZE ROAD**. This followed the line of the approach road to the abbey and is so marked on the Milward map of 1702, although there cannot have been much of the abbey left by that date. As late as 1835 this was the only road on the Priory site. By 1853 the road had been extended eastwards and was called St George's Terrace up to Priory Road and Upton Road from there to Abbey Road. In 1883 both names were abolished and Belsize Road came to Kilburn. **No. 221A** includes the old entrance to Kilburn High Road station on the LNWR, opened in 1852 and closed about 1923. Across the road an interesting group of buildings begins with **Priory Works**, dated 1892. This and the **arched area** adjoining it were first used as a furniture depository and later as a garage workshop, the name DUNLOP being picked out in the brickwork on the right-hand side. **No. 254** has had a varied life of public service, originating as the privately owned Kilburn Town Hall (1888), becoming the Theatre Royal (1896), adding Kilburn Empire to its title (1901) and later modulating to the Kilburn Picture Palace (1910). World War II put an end to its cinematic career, but it is now appropriately used by an audio-visual concern. The Post Office Sorting Office at **Nos. 260–2** closed in early 1991 after more than 100 years on the same site. Further east is the Victorian pub, **The Priory Tavern**; its landlord in the 1880s was called S.S. Death. Near the junction with Abbey Road, the active **Abbey Community Centre** began in 1975 and is expanding in all directions. Among its one thousand users per week are a Somali Group and the Kilburn Irish Youth Group, many of them newly arrived in this country.

HERMIT PLACE is a modern name recalling the recluse Godwin, who founded Kilburn Priory. This short road, now a string of garages, is nearly all that remains of Abbey Lane and **KILBURN VALE**, which in the mid-nineteenth century linked West End Lane and St George's Terrace. These narrow lanes have been replaced by the **Kilburn Vale Estate** (1948–1957). The **Ebenezer Baptist Chapel** (1870), now the Women's Missionary Fellowship, has survived in the Vale (the street name is on the chapel wall) and a **plaque** informs us that Thomas Creswick preached his last sermon at a bridge near here before his death on 31 August 1868. The nearby **KILBURN PLACE** is a non-residential cul-de-sac named in 1937.

To the north, **ABBOT'S PLACE**, linking West End Lane with Priory Road, was called Abbot's Road from about 1806 until 1939, when the LCC changed its name. **Nos. 1–6** are handsome Italianate originals with Venetian windows. The bungaloid **No. 10** was once the studio of 41 Priory Road.

PRIORY TERRACE was laid out about 1850, the houses being built by George Duncan and his son John. The road was called St George's Road until 1937, when the name was changed by the LCC. In 1899 Thomas J. Wise (1859–1937), the bibliophile and forger, was living in **No. 15** and in 1920 the *avant-garde* composer, Bernard van Dieren, was at **No. 35A**. In the same year the actor, Sir Dirk Bogarde, was born at **No. 39**: his father, Ulric van den Bogaerde, was Art Editor of *The Times*. In his memoirs Sir Dirk describes his birthplace as a 'grey elephant', but it is now one of the many well-decorated houses on the west side of the road. **Nos. 6–12** have attractive tondos in their gables. The artist Bernard Meninsky lived at **No. 23** from 1936–39 and the England cricketer, Jim Laker, was at **No. 30A** between 1953 and 1956.

Before leaving the Abbey Farm Estate, it is interesting to note that four mulberry trees reputedly marked the corners of the old Priory Estate. One was said to be in Quex Road, one in Boundary Road, a third in Springfield Lane and the fourth somewhere near St Mary's Church. Only the latter has been traced – to the garden of 196 Goldhurst Terrace.

To the north of this estate the southern tip of **WEST END LANE** narrows and idles in pleasant contrast to its busy northern sector. Near the small and recently refurbished **Bird in Hand** public house, one can still put an ear bravely to a **manhole cover** and hear the Kilburn stream rushing past below. This former river overflowed and rose to a height of three feet during the great storm of August 1975, as recorded on a **plaque** fixed to the wall of the pub. On Cruchley's map, this stretch of road is marked as Greville Cottages and later it was called Queen's Road, because of frequent visits here by Queen Victoria in search of country air. Mrs Barnes claims that it was not uncommon to see her walking in this part of West End Lane. In 1972 a house in the street, where luminous dials had been painted on clocks, became radio-active and had to be taken down brick-by-brick and buried twenty feet deep in a GLC dump at Harefield, Middlesex. **Nos. 26–30** catch the eye as original houses especially No. 28 with its pineapples. At the Kilburn High Road end, St Mary's Primary School was until recently crammed into a small scholastic backwater off the roaring mainstream. The school started in 1870 on the site of a dame school and was helped on its way by Major-General the Honorable Arthur Upton, the descendant and heir of Colonel Upton. The school moved to new premises on the corner of Quex Road and West End Lane in 1991. It was Major-General Upton who laid the foundation stone for St Mary's Church and was generally a benevolent landlord to the area.

THE EYRE ESTATE

The Eyre estate is associated with St John's Wood rather than with Hampstead, and the greater part indeed lies south of Boundary Road, which nowadays marks the southern limit of Hampstead and the London Borough of Camden. The estate came into the possession of the Eyre family in 1732, when Henry Samuel Eyre, a City merchant, bought the five hundred acres of the Earl of Chesterfield's St John's Wood estate for £20,000 mainly, it seems, to oblige the Earl, who urgently needed the money. The Earl held on to his Belsize estate, which he leased out to various shady characters, who turned Belsize House and grounds into notorious Pleasure Gardens (see *The Streets of Belsize*). At that time the Eyre estate consisted of wooded, meadow or pasture land and was divided by hedges into forty-five closes or fields. As agricultural land it was no gold mine. When a later Mr Eyre died in 1854 the total rent-roll was only £890 a year and apparently all the tenants were nearly two-and-a-half years in arrears.

The estate continued in the Eyre family, each generation producing a Henry Samuel Eyre. In the early nineteenth century, following the layout of the Regent's Park, the estate began to sprout fashionable villas. Although the Regent's ambition for a palace in the park was never realised, the interest aroused by the project was sufficient to draw many people to a home in the new suburb. Alan Montgomery Eyre, who wrote a history of St John's Wood in 1913, describes how in twenty years it 'became thickly peopled by authors, artists, Bohemians and *demi-mondaines*. Hither came the Landseers, the Leslies, Foscolo and the Hoggs, and the fame of St John's Wood largely took its character from these pioneers.'

The estate is bounded on the north by Belsize Road and the area lying within the old borough of Hampstead does not seem to have had the cachet of the part further south. There were few noteworthy residents and the houses were mostly built on a tighter scale, intended for less well-to-do people: these included many providing services, especially horse buses and small shops. Much of the area has been redeveloped since the last war and blocks of flats, both council and private, have replaced many of the earlier buildings.

Although **BOUNDARY ROAD** appears on a map of 1862 and the name was officially approved in 1868, it was not until 1900 that the border between the old parishes of Hampstead and St Marylebone was actually formed by the road. Prior to that, the parish boundary ran in a south-westerly direction from Finchley Road, and much of Springfield Road and the whole of Belgrave Road were included in Hampstead. (Boundary Road has remained in the NW8 postal district.) In the rationalisation of borough borders in 1900, the Greville Road area in the west was moved from St Marylebone to Hampstead. The stretch between Abbey and Bolton Roads was formerly called Grosvenor Road. The junction with Finchley Road is very roughly the site of the *strangraef* or stone pit mentioned as a Hampstead boundary mark in Ethelred's Charter of 986AD. Two of the old **boundary stones** can be seen at the Finchley Road end of Boundary Road, one in the wall on the north side and the other in the grounds of George Eliot School on the opposite side (together with a St Marylebone stone). Of the original houses, built in the spacious St John's Wood villa style, few now remain but an impression can be gained from **No. 7** (with its daring eagles) and **No. 9** which has since become madly Moorish. Sir Clement Freud, writer, *bon viveur* and MP, lived at No. 7 from 1953 to 1979. The residents towards the end of the century seem to have been middle-class professionals; in 1894 they included a surgeon, an architect, and three clergymen. At **No. 68** lived W.S. Hoyte (1844–1917), professor of organ at the Royal College of Music, whose pupils included Leopold Stokowski.

The Boundary Road houses on the Eyre estate to the east of Abbey Road had been built by 1853 and their condition had deteriorated to such an extent by 1937 that many were awaiting demolition. Redevelopment of the Hampstead side of the road began soon after World War II with the building of the **Ainsworth Estate**, presumably named after the novelist, Harrison Ainsworth who was once thought to have lived on the Hampstead side of Shoot-up Hill (*q.v.*). The blocks mostly commemorate nineteenth-century celebrities with local connections, including Walter Besant, Kate

Greenaway and Robert Louis Stevenson (see *The Streets of Hampstead*). **Stevenson House** is on the site of 94 Boundary Road, where the peripatetic Harmsworth family lived from about 1874 to 1888. Most of their eleven children went to Miss Budd's School next door and the boys progressed to Henley House in Mortimer Crescent (*q.v.*). At this time the future Lord Northcliffe enriched his school holidays by acting as cub reporter for the *Ham and High*. **AINSWORTH WAY** links the estate with Abbey Road and with the **Alexandra Priory School** and the **Jack Taylor School**.

The area between the Ainsworth Estate and the entrance to **BOUNDARY MEWS** was demolished in 1971. (Note the painted signs saying 'Commit No Nuisance' at the entry to the Mews.) At **No. 38A** Libris was opened in 1946 by an Austrian refugee, Joseph Suschitzky, and became the largest German-language bookshop in London. At **No. 38** the co-ownership flats **Dinerman Court** (named after Hampstead architect Freddy Dinerman) were opened in 1978. Helen Shapiro, singer and actress, lived at No. 30 Dinerman Court from 1978–1984. The empty space at **No. 36** marks the site of the Prince Arthur public house, which was licensed as a music hall from 1868 to 1871, when renewal was refused. At **No. 48** a Home for the Younger Physically Handicapped (architects: David Shalev and Eldred Evans) was opened in 1979. The original Victorian properties survive at **Nos. 20** to **34**. Included by the London Borough of Camden in 1979 in its plans for the final stage of the neighbouring Alexandra Road redevelopment, these shops were to have been replaced by old people's flats, a public house and a tenants' hall. In 1982 the then short-term residents, including several community organisations, successfully countered with their own proposals to rehabilitate the properties. Now converted to residential use, many features of the previous shop fronts can still be seen, including 'Boundary Road Stores' above **No. 32**, which was a grocer's for over a century. Between the wars, **No. 34** was Brewer's Bicycle Shop, the first in the area. To the west of Abbey Road, most of Boundary Road's original **shops** have survived.

On the corner with Abbey Road (**No. 83**) is the **Victoria** public house, which was also licensed as a music hall from 1856 to 1867. It was last rebuilt in 1963 and refurbished internally with assorted Victoriana in 1987. Next door at **No. 98A** Boundary Road, behind forbidding steel doors and security surveillance, is the **Saatchi Collection**. The former Victoria Yard on this site started life as one of the many local horsebus stables, in 1856 accommodating as many as 260 horses, and later became a depot for (private) motor buses. The present structure dates from the 1920s (with a northern addition in the 1950s) and was used first as a motor repair shop and until 1983 as a paint warehouse. The following year the buildings were converted by Max Gordon Associates for the Saatchis' modern art gallery, presenting selections from one of the world's largest collections of contemporary art.

Though entirely rebuilt in its northern stretch, **ABBEY ROAD** is one of the oldest in the district. Originally a footpath leading from London to Kilburn Priory, it is named after Westminster Abbey, to which the Priory belonged until the Dissolution. It is shown on Rocque's map of 1746 but was not developed until the next century. Houses started to be built at the south end, as shown on Cruchley's map of 1829, and by 1862 it was developed up as far as Boundary Road. It was in that year that **St Mary's Church**, on the corner of Priory Road, was consecrated. The architects were the brothers, F. and H. Francis, whose more exuberant commercial work was until recently to be seen at the corners of Northumberland Avenue and Trafalgar Square. The gothic-style St Mary's is the only church in West Hampstead to appear in the DoE Buildings List. Unlike several local churches, where the population arrived first and often had to make do with a temporary church for some years, this one preceded the building boom in the immediate area. The church itself was built on the assumed site of the nunnery of Kilburn and preserves a fragment of medieval brass from the Priory church. Set in the north transept, it shows the head of a nun who was possibly Emma de St Omer, the prioress in the days of Richard II. The stained glass in the chancel is by Clayton & Bell and a memorial window in the north aisle commemorates the organist (1920–46), R.J. Pitcher, and his invention, The Techniquer. This was a device to help novice organists to master the pedals but was not a commercial success. Pitcher was also a Professor of Singing at the Guildhall School of Music and had a scholarship at the Royal College of Music named after him.

Next to the church, six houses, **Nos. 124–134**, give an idea of the original residential style – semi-detached and semi-distinguished. These houses, together with the church, Priory Terrace and Priory Road (southern stretch) form a Conservation Area. To the south, redevelopment by the Council began in 1965 to create the **Abbey Estate**. **Casterbridge House** at the corner of Belsize Road commemorates Thomas Hardy's sojourn in Kilburn High Road (*q.v.*). Hardy, incidentally, worshipped at St Mary's for about a year. **Snowman House** recalls a mayor of Hampstead, who was also court jeweller to every monarch from Edward VII to Elizabeth II. Further blocks, **Mary Green** and **Emminster** also have Hardy names (but Marygreen was a place, not a person, in Hardy's novel). Incorporated in Emminster is the **Lillie Langtry** built in 1969 to replace another pub on this site, the Princess of Wales. (See below for a further local example of Princess Alexandra being ousted by her husband's mistress.) The brutal multi-storey **car park** opposite was built for council tenants but is little used as such; car sales and servicing and other workshops are now parked there instead. West of Abbey Road are more council blocks with names from the Wessex novels – **Exonbury** (Hardy's name for Exeter) and **Toneborough** (Taunton).

To the east is **BELSIZE ROAD**, one of the earliest east-west cross routes of the borough. (The western end is covered in Section Three.) The road is listed in the 1854 Directory and, as its name indicates, it led from Kilburn to the Belsize estate. In the early days the name Belsize Road was given only to the part between Finchley Road and the junction with Fairfax Road. Along with Hilgrove Road, the main part of Belsize Road was called Adelaide Road North, although 'West' might have been a more accurate description. As in other streets, parts were known by terraces or villas: Claremont Villas, Clarendon Terrace and Villas, and Princess Terrace existed until 1875, and the numbering was not finally sorted out until ten years later. In the first World War a Zeppelin dropped a bomb in the road and a quondam local resident recalls how she was thrown out of bed by the blast. A century ago the junction of Abbey and Belsize Roads was one of the few local Fixed Points for police, where a constable was permanently stationed from 9pm to 1am. The public was assured that 'in the event of any person springing a rattle or persistently ringing a bell in the street…the police will at once proceed to the spot and render assistance'.

One of the early builders in Belsize Road was Robert

26. Fragment of medieval brass in St Mary's, Kilburn.

ABBEY ROAD, ST. JOHN'S WOOD.

27. *The junction of Abbey Road and Belsize Road*, with the Princess of Wales pub (centre left).

Yeo, an assistant of Samuel Cuming, who later took over from him on the development of the Eton Estate (see *The Streets of Belsize*). On the north side the houses were built in rather cramped terraces but they have mostly kept their original decorations – window-sill pot-guards on **Nos. 152–170**, rustication and hairy heads on **Nos. 104–146** and balconettes and scallop shells on **Nos. 46–82**, which have been handsomely restored. On the south side **Nos. 115–129** are examples of the larger semi-detached villas. The remaining houses on this side, together with Barrett's Nursery (No. 67), were acquired and demolished by the LNWR. The blockish **blocks of flats** that replaced them were built between 1932 and 1962 and do not live up to their grand names, such as Rutherglen, Berkeley and Belvedere.

In the late 1880s, No. 164 was the home of Eugène ('Guggy') du Maurier, younger brother of the more famous George. Eugène's only claim to fame seems to have been that when in the French army he was demoted from the rank of corporal several times. To the east, **The Britannia** pub was moved round the roundabout from the Fairfax/Fairhazel corner in the early 1970s but kept its old name, taken from a local meadow. The road passes between the modern council estates and comes to a forlorn end; it has been blocked off where formerly it led to the arcaded entrance to **Swiss Cottage Station**. A little row of shops at this end called Swiss Terrace has disappeared and a new entrance to the station has been built. Current residents near here include Nora Beloff, noted author and foreign correspondent.

FAIRFAX ROAD, originally known as Victoria Road, was renamed in 1870, presumably as an early bicentenary tribute to General Fairfax (of no known Hampstead connection), who died in 1671. From association with the General's victories have sprouted **MARSTON CLOSE** and **NASEBY CLOSE** in the mid–1960s and both sides of Fairfax Road were neatly developed at the same time. The row of modern shops on the western side of Fairfax Road replaced earlier ones which provided for much more specialised needs; in 1888 they included a Berlin wool shop, a fancy repository, a straw hat manufacturer and a staymaker. The *South Hampstead Advertiser*, later incorporated in the *Hampstead News*, was published at the old No. 79 for several years from 1880, distributing eighty-three per cent of its copies free; it was therefore the area's first 'freebie'. A long-term resident at the old **No. 11** was John Clayton (1827–1913), partner in the stained glass firm of Clayton & Bell. At the beginning of this century, the old Britannia pub in Fairfax Road was a venue for local sporting organisations, including the Belsize Cricket Club, the Crescent Football and Cricket club, and St Mary's Gymnasium; members of the latter practised at St Mary's Hall, Abbey Road, and they reassured potential participants that the gym was not confined to church members but would welcome all 'who can produce evidence of respectability'.

This part of the Eyre estate became important for the provision of horse-bus stabling and termini, of which the largest was in Victoria Mews, later renamed Fairfax Mews and, after the departure of the horses, **FAIRFAX PLACE**. Some idea of the scale of operations can be gained on passing under the old **archway** next to No. 59, past the faded notice advocating the services of 'William Easun, Estd 1852, Builder, Decorator & Sanitary Engineer. Funerals Furnished'. A pair of cast-iron bollards by the archway are marked 'St John-at-Hampstead'. Fairfax Road's only surviving Victorian house is **No. 6**, at the corner with **HAR-BEN ROAD**, where the four attractive semi-detached houses, **Nos. 21–27**, are also the only original ones remaining. The writers John and Penelope Mortimer lived at No. 23 in the 1960s. Starting as Albion Road in the early 1850s, the street was renamed in 1937, in memory of Sir Henry Harben (1823–1911). Sir Henry was a member of the first LCC in 1889 and first Mayor of Hampstead in 1900 but he is best known locally for his contribution, as prime mover and donor, in securing Parliament Hill, Golders Hill Park and Fortune Green as public open spaces. A large scale memorial to him is the **Harben Estate**, occupying the north side of the road. **Dobson Close** is named after the painter W.C.T. Dobson, who lived in Adelaide Road. **Noel House**, **Campden House** and **Hickes House** all commemorate past Lords of the Manor of Hampstead.

HILGROVE ROAD was, as Adelaide Road North, built up in the 1850s at the same time as Belsize Road and as Adelaide Road itself. Only a few sad villas on the south side show its earlier pretentions. **Nos. 22** and **24** are built in high Victorian Gothic style, with pointed arches over the front doors and windows. The present street name dates from 1875 and seems to be merely descriptive: the road is certainly hilly but the grove, if any, must have disappeared a long time ago. The area is dominated by the large **Hilgrove Estate** which was built by the LCC in the late 1950s to accommodate 143 families. The development of flats and maisonettes was hailed by the *Ham and High* as 'yet another step in the transformation of Swiss Cottage from a bomb-scarred hotch-potch of shops and decaying houses to a busy modern centre, which people are already calling the Northern Gateway to London...'. An estate road is called **Dorman Way**. A tall sculpture in the grounds on the Finchley Road side is by Leon Underwood and entitled *Ideas*. In the 1890s **No. 20** was the home of Francis Tussaud,

28. *Loudoun Road*, c1910.

grandson of Madame Tussaud and an active wax-worker: several other members of the family lived in West Hampstead.

LOUDOUN ROAD crosses the old London North Western Railway, hence its earlier name of Bridge Road: the name was changed in 1871. Loudoun was also the name of a group of villas here before being adopted for the road name which presumably, despite the different Ayrshire spelling, refers to John Claudius Loudon (1783–1843). This well-known landscape gardener, writer and villa-builder lived in Bayswater and is buried at Kensal Green. He does not seem to have had any connection with Hampstead but perhaps the developers of the area borrowed ideas from his *Encyclopaedia of Cottage, Farm and Villa Architecture*, published in 1832.

All Souls' Church, whose parish was formerly part of St Paul's, Avenue Road, was consecrated in 1865. Like St Mary's, Abbey Road, it then stood near the northern fringe of development. It was the fruit of a brothers' partnership: Henry Robinson Wadmore was the instigator and its first vicar, a position he held until 1897, while his brother James was one of the architects. The tower was not added until 1905. The building's poor condition and the congregation's poor attendances led to the church being declared redundant in 1985. After a few years' use by the St John's Wood Liberal Synagogue during their rebuilding programme, the church's future is again uncertain. The parish was united with St Mary's, Kilburn, in 1990. In 1872 the parish school was built at the south end of Fairhazel Gardens (*q.v.*). Also in Loudoun Road is a monument to the early commuter age, **South Hampstead Station**. Originally built in 1879 as Loudoun Road Station, it was closed in 1917 as a wartime measure and reopened as South Hampstead in 1922 for the new electrified Watford-Euston service. There is a good view from here of the vast entrance to the **Primrose Hill Tunnel**, designed by Budden in 1835 for the London-Birmingham Railway and now a Listed Building.

Between the railway and Boundary Road, **ALEXANDRA ROAD** once ran all the way to Kilburn but the whole area has been redeveloped for council housing. A short stretch remains east of Loudoun Road and a few of the original four-storey houses still stand, now turned into flats. The road was built soon after the marriage of Princess Alexandra and the Prince of Wales in 1863. For a hundred years the road preserved its pleasant tree-lined appearance, its semi-detached houses stepped up from the road, built for the middle-class residents who named them, presumably,

after their holiday haunts: Purbeck House, Kendal Villa, Florence Villa, Sherborne House and so on. Ironically, the Kilburn end of the road has been renamed Langtry Road after a less respectable connection with the Prince of Wales. The most notorious resident of Alexandra Road, Mrs Lillie Langtry, became the Prince's mistress towards the end of the 1870s and he used to visit her here at Leighton House for 'a cup of tea'. The daughter of the Dean of Jersey, she had another very respectable relation and another local connection in her cousin, Philip le Breton, celebrated in Hampstead history for helping to save the Heath. Despite the lack of any acting talent, the beautiful 'Jersey Lily' later embarked on a successful stage career. While living in Alexandra Road she is reputed to have had twelve gallons of milk supplied for her bath daily by Lord Rayleigh's Dairies. Coincidentally, her second husband was called Sir Hugo de Bathe. Another much frequented house in this lost road was at the corner with Abbey Road where Mrs Dawson Scott brought writers together to found the PEN Club.

The redevelopment of Alexandra Road between Loudoun Road and Abbey Road began in 1972 and reached full occupancy by 1979. The road was pedestrianised and renamed **Rowley Way**, after Llewelyn Rowley, the Council's Housing Manager. Hailed as a 'high density success story', the concrete ziggurat-styled structure, likened by some to the Mappin Terraces of the Zoo, was among the largest council developments in Europe. But this 'Grand Canyon of NW6' was not popular with residents, mainly because of its (over)heating system. The terrace of shops to the east is called **Langtry Walk** and adjoins the new **Alexandra Place**.

THE MARYON WILSON ESTATE

The Maryon Wilsons owned the largest estates in Hampstead as befitted their feudal sounding title, Lords of the Manor, still extant in the twentieth century. Their 416 acres were in two blocks – 60 acres alongside the Heath and 356 acres in a stretch to the west and south-west of the old village of Hampstead. These lands had been in the possession of the family since Sir Thomas Spencer Wilson married the great-niece of John Maryon, heir to the manor of Hampstead, in 1767. The story of the family battle to develop their estates in the nineteenth century is told in detail by Thompson. It was not until 1874 that development of south and west Hampstead at last got under way.

Priory Road was the first to be built, then Canfield and Broadhurst Gardens and Goldhurst Terrace were started in the second half of the 1870s, Compayne, Greencroft and Fairhazel Gardens from 1885–95, and finally Aberdare Gardens in the later 1890s. Predominant especially in the earlier roads are the red brick mansion flats, often with turrets on the corner blocks. This was the period when such purpose-built flats for the middle classes started to be built in many parts of London and they proved popular with single people, widows and small families living on fairly restricted means. The rather grandiose name of 'mansions' shows that they had distinctly stylish pretensions and, while their occupants were not 'carriage folk', they normally kept a resident maid. Not visible from the street are the large, very pleasant communal gardens behind the blocks, justifying the names of the roads and compensating for the lack of any local public open space.

PRIORY ROAD marked the boundary between the Maryon Wilsons' estate and that of their neighbour, Colonel Cotton, and had existed as a footpath, connecting Hampstead with Kilburn Priory, for many years. The two landowners agreed to straighten the line of the footpath and to share the cost of making up the new road. Originally it was known as Canfield Road but perhaps Colonel Cotton objected to a name from Maryon Wilson territory and in 1880 it was redesignated, neutrally, after the old Priory. St Mary's Church (see Abbey Road) is the largest building here. **No. 50** next door was its vicarage from 1877 to 1983 but has now become flats. (A new vicarage was built in the garden next to the church hall.) Behind Nos. 52 and 54, **St Mary's Mews** was created and occupied in 1978. The houses in this stretch of the road were built in 1876/7 over the local cricket ground, despite much protest from the gentlemen and players. Hampstead's cricket club, formed in 1867, used to play on a ground near Primrose Hill and was known as the St John's Wood Cricket Club: it moved to

West Hampstead in 1871. Across Abbey Road, **No. 48** was taken over in 1895 as the Kilburn Branch Library. The first Public Library in Hampstead, it moved to Cotleigh Road in 1901. By the 1890s it was a well established and obviously very respectable neighbourhood. Residents included a barrister, a surgeon, a professor of music and two private schools. Hesketh Pearson, author and critic, noted for his biographies of Oscar Wilde and Bernard Shaw, lived at **No. 14** from 1950–1964. This house and its neighbour have handsome swagging and, like adjoining houses, have kept their decorative pot-guards. This southern stretch of Priory Road has a grand air, with white four-storey houses and square corner towers. To the north, there are some occasional pleasures, **No. 78** and its neighbours have fleur-de-lys and swags; **No. 98** sports a weathervane and ornate chimney pots and **No. 107**, an old coach house, has kept its cupola.

At the north end of the estate, **BROADHURST GARDENS** was named after a farm on the Sussex estate of the Maryon Wilsons. It roughly follows the course of an old path known as Gypsy Lane, which linked the Belsize and Kilburn ends of Hampstead. Building started from the east and by 1887 it was numbered through to West End Lane. The road suffered considerable bomb damage in the last war, especially on the north side, presumably because of its proximity to the railways. The bomb sites were bought by the LCC in 1947 and a large number of **flats** (architect: Richard Nickson) were completed by 1956. At the west end, **No. 165**, now called Lilian Baylis House because of its tenure by the English National Opera, began life in 1884. It was built by Thomas Bate as the Falcon Works and adorned in its pediment with a castle and an eagle. As this is the seal of the borough of Bedford and Mr Bate was a Devon man,

29. *West Hampstead Town Hall*, Broadhurst Gardens, 1912.

30. *Walter Sickert*, by Max Beerbohm, *c*1912.

it seems probable that he just liked the design and mistook an eagle for a falcon. After three empty years, the building was bought by a local butcher, H.G. Randall, licensed as a temporary church (St James's, Sherriff Road, was imminent) and by April 1888 turned into a private entertainments centre known as West Hampstead Town Hall. In 1933 it was being used by the Crystalate Gramophone Recording Company and four years later by the newly formed Decca Company: they moved to the old Kilburn Town Hall in 1987. Among the small shops at this end of the road is a terrace called **Broadwell Parade**.

WEST HAMPSTEAD MEWS was built as stabling in 1884 but the impressive coach house in the south-west corner is dated two years later. The coat of arms, with its lion rampant and motto *Beneficiorum Memor*, presumably belonged to the coach's owner, Colonel Saner, a resident of Chislett Road, who came from Hull. Baines commends his 'ripe discernment' as a local JP and his energetic support in the building of St James's. The adjoining **EXETER MEWS** was a later development.

Back in Broadhurst Gardens and past the railway **footbridge** (see Granny Drippen's Steps) **Nos. 109–15** have unusual design and No. 109 has kept its original name, Hazelwood, from the 1890s. Note the hefty stone bear between Nos. 113–15, supporting the roof parapet. **No. 97**, now a block of luxury flats, has its date 1891 over the door. On the site of **Broadfield** (south side) was No. 69, which early this century was the home of the self-styled Baron Corvo. His real name was Frederick Rolfe and he is most remembered now for his eccentricity and for his engaging novel, *Hadrian VII* (1904). Among other demolished houses, No. 98 was until 1928 a preparatory school for boys, York House; No. 54 was from 1885–94 the home of artist Walter Sickert, founder of the Camden Town Group, and No. 34 the address of a lesser known artist, John Henry Henshall. **No. 31** was the Sarah Klausner Memorial Synagogue from 1947 to the early 1970s. At **No. 1**, a large house still standing on the corner of Greencroft Gardens, lived Madame Bergman-Osterberg, a pioneer of physical education in this country. She came here in the 1880s and opened her Hampstead Gymnasium and Physical Training College, which won much acclaim. Apart from introducing Swedish drill, she popularised the gym slip throughout the country, despite protests from older gymnasts that it was 'wickedly short'. In about 1900, alarmed by threats of railway developments on her doorstep, she moved to Dartford and continued her PE activities there. A plaque to Madame Bergman-Osterberg has disappeared from the house in Broadhurst Gardens but round the corner can still be seen her glass-domed hall, dated 1885, where gymnastics flourished under other auspices until World War II. Thereafter, apart from a spell as the Jewish Art Centre, the athletic tradition has been continued here by various exotically-named dance clubs.

COMPAYNE GARDENS was the name originally given only to the part of the road between Canfield Gardens and Priory Road. West of that, on the Powell-Cotton Estate, it was, until 1937, known as Chislett Road, after a property in Kent belonging to the family. The origin of Compayne is not known; there is no evident link with Compiegne, where Joan of Arc was taken prisoner. The road developed from the east and it was at this end that T.S. Eliot lived in 1915/16 with the Haigh Wood family at **No. 3**. He and Vivien, the daughter of the house, were married at Hampstead Town Hall in June 1915. Another man of distinction, though not a household name, lived at **No. 28** in the 1950s:

31. *T.S. Eliot* by Wyndham Lewis.

32. *The Turret, 82 Compayne Gardens*, drawn by its architect, Banister Fletcher.

he was John Rex Whinfield, the inventor of terylene. This is one of many houses hereabouts that has a carved face over the entrance. At the junction with Fairhazel Gardens, **Ranworth** (a Broads name) and **Compayne Mansions**, dated 1893 and 1894 respectively, are in their rather ponderous red brick. Note also the Victorian **pillar box**. A private blue plaque on **No. 43** records that 'Dr Nahum Sokolow, Statesman and Author, President of the World Zionist Organisation, lived and worked here from 1921–1936'. He called the house Hazephirah. Another plaque may well go up on **No. 68**, where the conductor Sir Adrian Boult came to live in 1977 and died in 1983. The present **No. 74**, Princess Court, has replaced the home of the Bolivian Consul General, who lived here at the turn of the century and called it Santa Cruz: its fashionable atmosphere is evoked in *My Bolivian Aunt*, written by his wife's nephew, Cecil Beaton. Another consul lived across the road in the 1880s and '90s: the house was called Highfield, on the site of **No. 73**, and the consul was Belgian. The present house has belonged since about 1938 to the Maccabi Association, whose new buildings were opened by Princess Anne in 1972. This end of Compayne Gardens is in a different estate and has a grander look: the houses, all built in the 1880s, have an individual dignity and style. **No. 82** was originally known as the The Turret and was designed by the revered Banister Fletcher senior. He owned and probably designed several other nearby houses with similar gateposts and porches, while based in Woodchurch Road (*q.v.*) himself. These include **No. 75**, first called Gothic House, and **No. 80** and the rather grand **No. 84** (Redruth and Ladywell). **White Friar's Court** takes its name from the original house on this site. Different faiths have flourished at **No. 88**, now labelled Zoroastrian House.

It was built in 1886 for a Quaker, Silvanus P. Thompson, pioneering physicist, scientific and theological author, who lived there until his death in 1916. From 1922 this was St Dominic's Convent and school for young ladies and from 1934 it was St Mary's RC School run by Sisters of Charity. Since 1969 it has belonged to the Zoroastrians, followers of the ancient religion of Persia, founded by the prophet Zorathustra, the first proponent of Monotheism. Their New Year Festival on 21 March may bring some 600 people to No. 88.

This part of West Hampstead was clearly a developer's estate, as the major roads were all laid out neatly parallel with each other. **CANFIELD GARDENS** is named after the Maryon Wilson seat in Essex. Here mansion flats predominate, with rural names like **Ellesmere** (dated 1889) and **Maisiemore**, named and dated (1886) on a brick arch. More dates appear on **Wroxham** (1890) and **Redesdale Mansions** (1887) and the latter has a Victorian **pillar box** outside. **3 Stirling Mansions** was, from 1920–26, the home of Sir Selwyn Selwyn-Clarke KBE, a former Governor of the Seychelles and, nearer home, President of the Hampstead division of the Red Cross. Peter Wishart, the versatile composer, lived at **1 Pembroke Mansions** between 1964–69. One of the first two women members of the LCC, Miss E.J. Cobden, daughter of the famous Richard Cobden, was an early resident at **No. 17** Canfield Gardens. An attempt to unseat her from the LCC because of her sex was at first successful but later foiled. The artists John Robert Dicksee and his son, Herbert Thomas, were living at **Nos. 87** and **36** respectively in the 1890s: his nephew, another of five Dicksees, who all exhibited at the Royal Academy, was a near neighbour. Until recently, the popular nonagenarian novelist, Lettice Cooper, lived at **No. 95**. Current residents in the street include the film and theatre director, Lindsay Anderson. The part of the road west of Fairhazel Gardens has solid brick houses with little decoration except their wrought-iron balconies. These were built a little later and originally called Canfield Gardens West. The whole road was renumbered in the early 1890s. Sandwiched between the railway lines next to Finchley Road station is **CANFIELD PLACE**, originally built as a mews containing livery stables for the estate. These buildings were pulled down in the 1890s to make way for railway extensions and, when the mews was rebuilt, much of the stabling was not replaced. Some haylofts are still visible, however. John Barnes, the Finchley Road store, used to keep their van horses here and one of their warehouses has recently been transformed into a mews of offices.

GREENCROFT GARDENS is named after another farm near Great Canfield in Essex. Building started from Broadhurst Gardens and had reached Fairhazel Gardens by 1886. The part between Priory Road and Fairhazel Gardens was originally Westcroft Road: it was renamed by 1894. The whole road was renumbered in 1897, following a complaint by the Superintendent Architect of the LCC of the 'inconvenience caused by peculiar numbering'. Lindsay Anderson (see above) lived at **No. 57** in the 1960s and '70s. **No. 62** has its date (1888) over the door. The road has an austere look but, west of Fairhazel Gardens, there are some attractive wrought-iron canopies and, further along, there are some pleasant surprises. **Nos. 103–17** and **Nos. 114–128** are handsomely decorated with ornate oriels and cornices. Saul Isaac, who lodged at **No. 109** in Edwardian times, achieved some fame as the first Jew to be elected as a Conservative MP and as a member of the Carlton Club: he was MP for Nottingham 1874–80 and had made his money as an army contractor in the American Civil War.

The name of **GOLDHURST TERRACE** was taken from a wood on the Maryon Wilson Estate in East Sussex and approved in 1877. At first it was divided into Goldhurst Terrace West and East and was renumbered outwards in both directions from Fairhazel Gardens. With obvious justification the residents complained and the whole road was renumbered in 1896 from Finchley Road to Priory Road. In 1897 residents in the western part complained again, this time about the unfinished condition of the road. It was a hard time for the pioneers of West Hampstead. John Barnes & Company established themselves at 2 Goldhurst Terrace in 1899. In recent years an antique shop, **No. 1** was a Customs & Excise Office in 1917–19. About this time, the artist, Walter Bayes, a founder member of the Camden Town Group and the London Group, lived at **No. 45**. Lower down the road, two modern blocks resulted from bombing in the last war – Maryon House and Wilson House. At the north-west end in **No. 194**, once called the Priory, the sculptor Arthur Glover was resident from 1929–40: he was a regular exhibitor at the Royal Academy. **No. 196** was originally called 'Ivor' and was built in 1881 (date above main door) for one Vitruvius Wyatt.

The last infill in this area was **ABERDARE GARDENS**, not completed until the end of the century. It was probably named after Henry Bruce, first Baron Aberdare, who was Home Secretary from 1868–73 and a popular reformer of the licensing laws: he died in 1895 when the road was being built. **No. 2** has been the Provincial House of the Sisters of Hope since 1960. The writer Dannie Abse lived at **No. 38** from 1943 until he qualified as a doctor in 1950. **No. 64** was the home of the architectural historian, Professor Reyner Banham, in the 1970s: he is said to have invented the term 'Pop Art'.

FAIRHAZEL GARDENS runs north west to south east, connecting many of these roads. It was named after a Sussex property of the Maryon Wilsons and follows the line of a footpath, shown on the 1866 OS map. In its early days it was known as North End Road and was chiefly used for access to the horse bus stables in Fairfax Mews. The children of the bus drivers were originally taught in a local hayloft but in 1872 a school was built for them near Belsize Road, which today is used as the **Afro-Caribbean Day Centre**. The school was originally run by All Souls' Church, Loudoun Road, and had room for 194 pupils. It was closed by the LCC in 1951 and became a Civil Defence Training Centre and until 1990 the Hampstead HQ of the Red Cross.

Fairhazel Gardens was built in the earlier stage of development of the estate and for a time was the western boundary of Compayne, Canfield and Greencroft Gardens. This is apparent from the change in building styles on either side. Most of the blocks of mansion flats lie in the roads to the east, while to the west are the later detached and semi-detached houses, built when this part of West Hampstead was acquiring a higher social tone. The road suffered severe damage in the last war, especially at the south end, but has mostly been rebuilt. Large open spaces still exist, however behind the houses to the east; and next to **No. 48** is the entrance to some thriving **allotments**. **COLERIDGE GARDENS** was formerly a mews, named after the poet who was a frequent visitor to Hampstead and perhaps strolled across the fields of West Hampstead while courting the muse. If he strolled now into this light industrial enclave, which was last replanned in 1983, he would get quite a shock.

Up Finchley Road

...But here we are in the Finchley Road
With drizzling rain and a skidding 'bus
And the twilight settling down on us.

So wrote Ford Madox Ford in his poem *Finchley Road*, first published in 1910, soon after the author had had a nervous breakdown and taken lodgings here. **FINCHLEY ROAD** was the brainchild of Colonel Henry Samuel Eyre, owner of the rich St John's Wood Estate (see Section Four), which he was developing around 1820. He had much to gain by launching an individual turnpike trust for the building of this grand new road to Finchley, but unexpected opposition came from Sir Thomas Maryon Wilson, Lord of the Manor of Hampstead. Among other objections he feared that his tenants' privacy would be 'disturbed and diminished if, by a new Road, as designed, the idle or pleasurable (not to say vicious) members of any portion of the Metropolis are to be drawn to Hampstead for objects of pleasure or crime...' He was, of course, worried about the value of his land but all his efforts to stop the new road (well detailed by Thompson) were defeated by an Act of Parliament in 1826. The building of Finchley New Road soon began and was completed by 1835. (When it reaches Finchley it is called Regent's Park Road, but our survey finishes on the Hampstead border at Hendon Way.)

'It promises to be the most imposing avenue or public highway near London', says Baines, noting that it has been newly planted (1889) with sycamore, elm and plane trees and that it would 'in a few years be an attractive, perhaps even a stately thoroughfare'. Whatever attractions the road had were rudely removed by the widening schemes of the 1960s. On the completion of this six-lane highway in 1969, the Royal Institute of British Architects commented: 'It is a very difficult and dangerous road. We are in a hostile environment...The buffer of plane trees has been swept away, with the result that the road has become a dirty, cold and fume-laden tunnel...'. The vicar of Holy Trinity regretted also that his parish had been divided in two by 'a sort of barrier reef'.

Before the 1960s most of the original houses had anyhow disappeared, including the grand residences of artist Burton Riviere at No. 82 and of the successful landscape painter, Yeend King, at No. 103. One of the survivors, though much rebuilt and extended, was the (Ye Olde) **Swiss Cottage Tavern**, which is first mentioned in the Rate Books of 1840. The fashion for chalets in this country dates back to about 1815, when Sir Jeffry Wyatville designed one for the

33. *Swiss Cottage* panorama in the 1890s, with (L-R) Avenue Road, Finchley Road and Belsize Road.

Duke of Bedford at Endsleigh in Devon. The first Swiss Cottage in London was built in the grounds of the Colosseum in Regent's Park between 1829 and 1832 by the architect P.F. Robinson. This architectural trend was boosted by an opera, *Le Chalet*, by Adolphe Adam (of *Giselle* fame), staged in Paris in 1834. Little wonder then, that the new Tavern at the start of Finchley Road and at the junction with six other roads was in the popular style. The Swiss Cottage gave its name to an area which grew in importance when it acquired a bus terminus in 1856 and a station on the Underground (then Metropolitan) in 1868. Baines reported in 1890 that the pub was a noted meeting place for 'running men', who ran races in Finchley Road. Until 1873 it had also refreshed travellers pausing here to pay their fees at the Junction Road Toll Gate before using this grand new road.

The remainder of the central island at Swiss Cottage was

redeveloped in the late 1930s. The **Odeon**, which was the No. 1 cinema on the Odeon circuit, was opened in 1937, then in 1973 converted into a triple-screen show-place by Rank. Recently a major rebuilding scheme has been mooted. The **Regency Lodge** flats by R. Atkinson, which were erected in 1938, have relief panels decorated with builders' tools.

The area to the east of Avenue Road has an impressive record of public service. **Swiss Cottage Library** is on the site of a large Congregational chapel built in 1851 and belonging to the nearby New College (*q.v.*). To the north was a hospital, first called Sunnyside and later St Columba's, which moved to Spaniards Road in 1956. At the corner with College Crescent was a Blind School which survived from the 1860s to the last war. All this area was cleared by Hampstead Borough Council in the 1950s to be developed into a new Civic Centre. With Sir Basil Spence as their architect, the Council completed the Library and **Sports Centre** in 1964 and these were opened by the Queen. (The Library's vertical decor represents the leaves of a book, while the horizontal lines of the Sports Centre, previously known as the Baths, are waves.) Further plans were complicated by the coming of Camden in 1965. After much discussion, part of the site was sold to London and Paris Holdings in 1981, resulting in the **office block** at the north-west corner, designed by Ted Levy, Benjamin & Partners, and in an **open space** known by some as Swiss Cottage Green. Currently on the site are such useful institutions as a **Citizens' Advice Bureau** (under financial threat), a **Community Centre** (see *The Streets of Belsize*) and a **Market Square**. After a number of false starts in the 1970s, the market was officially opened (by Alan Bennett) in 1985, with profits going to the Community Centre and the Winchester youth project next door. A market sign says: 'We are here to add sparkle to your weekend'. The **Hampstead Theatre Club**, which had begun under James Roose-Evans in 1959 at the Moreland Hall, was relocated at Swiss Cottage in 1962. It moved to its present tiny premises in 1967 and was soon appealing for funds for such amenities as air-conditioning (slogan 'Pay Now, Breathe Later'). Many of its recent productions have won awards and transferred to the West End. The bronze abstract **sculpture** outside the front of the Library is by Frederick McWilliam in 1964 and called *The Hampstead Figure*. Tucked away at the rear is a bronze **statue** by Nemon of the Father of Psychoanalysis, Sigmund Freud. A local resident in 1938/9, he is shown in pensive mood, as well he might be, surrounded by such streams of traffic.

The southern stretches of Finchley Road were totally rebuilt after the last war. The development of the Hilgrove Estate (*q.v.*) swept away all the Victorian villas on the western side. **No. 121** is on the site of the long-established building firm of C. Tavener and Son, who left in 1971. Next to **Cresta House**, built in the early 1980s, steps lead down to **Swiss Cottage Tube Station**, which, after a Metropolitan period and from 1940 a Bakerloo period, has been on the Jubilee Line since 1979. There has been a bank at **No. 135** for over a century but **Centre Heights** next door only arose in 1961, designed by Douglas Stephen and Panos Koulermos. The new **shops** have replaced the original villas here including No. 143, which was a well-known boys' preparatory school called Peterborough Lodge: its grounds stretched right down to Harben Road. During the last war the Viennese Theatre Club (*Das Laternl*) flourished on the site of **No. 151** and next door was the Circle of International Art. Further shops here are called **Harben Parade** (see Harben Road) and above are council flats, **Harrold House**. A plaque on the front pays tribute to Philip Henry Harrold OBE, who was the Town Clerk of Hampstead from 1931 to 1956.

On the eastern side, Finchley Road begins with a succession of post-war parades. **Regency Parade** (on the island) is followed by **Northways** and **New College Parades**, the latter commemorating a theological establishment on this site between 1850 and 1934: it has left its name also on College Crescent. An oasis of **greenery** at the corner with College Crescent includes the tree planted in 1953 to mark the coronation of Elizabeth II (see plaque on pavement). This must be one of the most polluted oases in London. The **Cosmo Restaurant** opened at 4–5 Northways Parade in 1938 and its menu and decor (and some of its clientele also?) have changed little since.'In its time', wrote Ruth Gorb recently in the *Ham and High*, 'it has been a mecca for

34. Turn-of-the-century picture of *Finchley Road*, showing (L-R) John Barnes, the Metropolitan Station and Holy Trinity.

local literati and a haven, just like home, for refugees from Nazi Germany'. The Cosmo café next door recently won a *Time Out* award for the best breakfast in London. Further refreshment can be found at the **North Star**, which opened its bars in 1850 and has kept its original starry facade, including a handsome balcony.

The steep slope of **TRINITY WALK** leads to Maresfield Gardens and from 1939 was known as Maresfield Path. The present name was adopted in 1977 to help deliveries to the path's only buildings, the villagey-looking **Holy Trinity School**. This C of E primary school originated in Belsize Lane in 1872 and came here four years later to be nearer its parent church. The present **Holy Trinity Church**, consecrated in 1978, is on the site of the 1872 version, developed from a thriving mission hall in Belsize Lane. In the 1970s, the congregation moved temporarily to a converted funeral parlour higher up Finchley Road, while their new church,

together with offices and flats, **Alban House**, were built on the old site. These flats are also approached by **Sumpter Close**.

North of Fairfax Road on the western side, **Fairfax Mansions** herald a rather grander late-Victorian Parade. **Nos. 167–175** have rewarding features including ornamental drainpipes. Lessiters have been at 167A since World War I and claim to be one of the oldest shops in London making hand-made chocolates. Another long-established business was Joseph Moody, gentlemen's hosier, hatter and shirtmaker, who opened at No. 171A in 1885 and closed in 1977. The present shop (DuDu) retains some of his splendid mahogany fittings and an imposing flight of stairs. Sainsbury's opened at No. 177 in 1973, following a smaller version higher up the road (from 1894) and preceding a bigger version back up the road (from 1994?). The first enterprise at No. 177 was the Swiss Cottage Skating Rink, which gave way in 1887 to Hampstead's first Public Baths and Gymnasium. These closed in 1964 when this healthy business was transferred to Swiss Cottage. **Nos. 179–189** include Marlborough House, which has had the honour to house the *Ham and High's* editorial department since 1988.

The one-acre island site fronting **Nos. 191–217** (now Habitat and Waitrose) was taken in 1900 by John Barnes's department store, replacing 14 shops called Fitzjohns Parade. The new store seemed luxuriously large, including its telegraphic address, Jonbarnaco-Swiss. Mr John Barnes, the first chairman of directors, was drowned in a shipwreck before the original building was finished. In 1926 the business came under the control of Selfridge's and in 1940 it joined the John Lewis Partnership. The new building, topped by the **St John's Court** flats, was opened in 1936, designed by Sir Thomas Bennett. It is basically in the popular ocean-liner style of the period but peppered with polygonal bay windows. The Mayor of Hampstead claimed that the new building would make Finchley Road 'the Regent Street of North London'. John Barnes closed in 1981.

Further north, **Canfield House** is richly decorated with swags of fruit and cherubs in pseudo-chateau style: it was erected in 1914–15 when **Finchley Road Station**, itself quite handsome up top, was rebuilt to designs by Frank Sherrin (completed by Allan & Co.). The original station opened in 1879 as part of the Metropolitan and St John's Wood Railway and was joined by the Bakerloo Line in 1940. The tall terrace of **Nos. 223–265**, which sports some leafy panels, was previously known as Fitzjohns Promenade and is still so named above No. 223. This was dominated in the 1880s by the drapers, Symmons Brothers, who styled their premises 'The Louvre' (no less) and, from the turn of the century, by other outfitters, Green and Edwards. Older residents fondly recall the latter's overhead change-machine system. Note the painted sign on the end wall of No. 265 for Lewis & Burrows Ltd, a long-established chemist (until 1921) at this address. But this will soon disappear as all this frontage (from *c*Nos. 241–279) is due to make way for the Finchley Centre. The eleven acre site, which stretches back to West End Lane, will eventually house a £100 million shopping centre, leisure centre and flats. Included in the demolition will be the shops of **Midland Crescent**, which marked the entrance to an earlier Finchley Road Station, opened on the Midland Railway in 1868. This followed the remarkable engineering feat of building the Belsize tunnel, which brought the Midland Line from Bedford through to the new St Pancras. Hundreds of navvies worked day and night to dig this mile-long tunnel and line it with twenty-two million bricks, many of which were made locally from the excavated clay. The station, shown as Finchley Road & St John's Wood Station in the 1926 Directory – perhaps to improve its image – bowed to competition in the following year and closed for passenger traffic.

Back on the east side, next to No. 130 a **seat** commemorates C.P. Munn, a builder long based in Hampstead (see below) and one-time president of the local Rotary club. In the 1890s the eleven following shops were known as the Esplanade. In front of **Frognal Court**, built in 1934, **Frognal Parade** is a terrace of shops, which once included such useful institutions as the Invisible Mending Co. (stocking ladders cost 3d each). At the old No. 158 was one of Hampstead's first cinemas, the Frognal Bijou Picture Palace, which flourished (under various titles) from 1911 to 1930. Next door at **No. 160** (now grandly double-fronted) was in the 1920s the Hampstead Palais de Danse. North of Frognal, there are a few original decorated facades. **Arkwright**

Mansions is pleasantly ornate with its pillars and balconies and a dome to echo the top-knot of the nearby Camden Arts Centre (for which, see *The Streets of Hampstead*).

Some of the buildings on the other side of Finchley Road can also be enjoyed for their decorations including **No. 289** which has 'Fullers Chocolates Sweets Cakes Teas' painted in red on the south side. One of two side turnings, **ROSE-MONT ROAD** was developed in the 1890s and its name appears to be just a pretty one. (It could commemorate a village near Dublin.) The buildings originated as livery stables, which then gave way to garages and small businesses. Some of the hayloft openings are still visible. **No. 4** was a Training Centre for the Blind in the late 1930s. **LITHOS ROAD** was evidently christened by a developer who knew the Greek for 'stone': the parish stoneyard was located here from 1880. The site was taken over for the vestry's Electricity Works in 1894 and Hampstead proudly became the second vestry in London to establish a municipal electricity supply. As a trade paper said at the time: 'It may be presumed that the wealthy residents of Hampstead will enjoy the luxury of electric lighting and that the artistic element in the population will welcome it in preference to gas'. The vestry supply was also preferred to the efforts of such private enterprises as the Hampstead Battery Company, run by local builders and property owners. The Lithos Road Works were eventually absorbed into the London Electricity Board and became a familiar address for local electricity bills. The L.E.B. left in 1986 and the works have been demolished. Vast numbers of flats are now being built here by the council and Housing Associations. Blocks named already include Banyan, Iroko and 'Sandal-wood (formerly Sycamore)'. Lithos Road was built up between 1873 and 1896 on the site of brickfields, which were

also a rubbish dump. The houses are decorated brick and the mansion blocks have attractive names like Claremont, Gainsboro and Jesmon Dene. But the area has long been threatened with change and decay, as the Council's Central Hampstead Redevelopment Scheme hangs over it. The building at the north corner with Finchley Road has its date 1891 and decorative initials WHS: these stand for W. Hill and Son, who were bakers and confectioners here.

From the 1890s this Finchley Road frontage was called Fitzjohns Pavement. This stretched from No. 293 to the **footpath** to West Hampstead, usually called locally the Black Path (why?). After some years as a funeral parlour, **No. 295** became Holy Trinity's temporary home in the 1970s (see above). **No. 317**, with a fine mural on its north end wall, has had a varied career, housing a dairy, motor engineers, estate agents and, from the 1950s, C.P. Munn, the builder (*q.v.*). It has only been a pub since 1969 and the present O'Henery's is its third title (from the late 1980s). Of the three local stations, **Finchley Road and Frognal**, now part of the North London Link, was the first in the field. In fact when it opened on the Hampstead Junction Railway in 1860, it was literally in the middle of open country. At the turn of the century the old Nos. 325–7 were the home and studios of the artistic Forsyth family. Two called James (?father and son) were sculptors and one named John was a stained glass painter: all exhibited frequently at the Royal Academy. John designed three windows for the chapels in Hampstead Cemetery.

No. 337 stands out has having been well built (1880s) and well restored (it was for long a doctor's surgery), while **No. 339** has been much altered and not for the better. It began grandly as the International College in 1885, designed in 'a free adaptation of the Gothic' by the distinguished local architect, Banister Fletcher senior (see Woodchurch Road). The original building had a tower containing an astronomical observatory, dormitories for some 100 boarders and a hall to seat 800 scholars. The college's promoter and principal was James Haysman, who had already opened the Anglo-French College in Burgess Park (see below): both institutions were run on his System of International Education, which stressed the value of learning modern languages. Another of his creeds was that 'the commerce of Great Britain should be carried on by British youths and not by imported Germans'. The college left Finchley Road in 1907 and the building was then divided into smaller units.

Above Lymington Road, the old No. 343 was Langfier Court Photographers from 1895 until it was blasted by a bomb in 1941. (The firm's story is told in *Camden History Review* No. 15.) Tall aerials atop **No. 361** mark a British Telecom building in Palladian style, which from 1932 to 1985 was the Hampstead Telephone Exchange. **Mandeville Court** next door was briefly the refuge of the artist, Oskar Kokoschka, soon after fleeing from Austria in 1938. Other mansion blocks catch the eye. **Dunrobin Court** has a plaque saying 1928. On the other side, **Langland** and **Leinster Mansions** have similar turrets. Dutch gables creep in around **No. 230** and this frontage hides a remarkable private open space of 2 acres, contained in the triangle with Langland Gardens and Frognal Lane. The peripheral houses once belonged to the Worshipful Company of Clothworkers.

Above the green-spired **St Andrew's Church** (note foundation stone of 1903), the houses tend to be heavy Victorian residences. An exception is the Council's **Studholme Court**, named after an Edwardian theatrical beauty, Marie Studholme, who once lived in the road. A leafy path, **Croftway**, follows an old right of way from here to Ferncroft Avenue. On the west side, the vast **Avenue Mansions** have attractive turrets and cupolas on the corner with Cannon Hill. **No. 519** and **No. 525** have curious decorations and the latter has a plaque AD 1887 over its side entrance. The imposing **Parsifal College** is now the London Regional Centre of the Open University, to which the dates graven in stone over its entrance 'Founded 1803, Rebuilt 1887' do not apply. They relate to its predecessor on this site, New College, which in fact traced its origins back to the Harmondsworth Charity of 1673. With this and other funds, dissenting divinity students were enabled to enjoy an Oxbridge-style education. There developed a number of alliterative academies at Homerton, Highbury and Hackney, which achieved a final aspiration by coming together in Hampstead. From 1900 the college became one of the Divinity Schools of London University, enlarged in 1934 by students from the other New College at Swiss Cottage (*q.v.*). Behind the 1887 block by M.P. Manning is the 1934 'New Building' by G.C. Lawrence and Partners. The premises, which were used by the Women's Royal Naval Service in the last war, were vacated by the college in 1977 and immediately adopted by the Open University. Next door **No. 527A** was built as the West Hampstead Congregational Church by Spalding and Cross in 1894, was sold to the Shomrei Hadath Synagogue in 1947 and is now under development for luxury flats, to be called The Octagon. (The synagogue has a new building round the corner.)

After a number of unexpected 1930s detached houses with bow fronts, **Nos. 551–573** offer a good ironwork balcony over the shops and the inevitable turret at the corner with Fortune Green Road. At the turn of the century, this terrace was known as Burgess Parade. There was a bank at **No. 575** from the 1920s, which presumably explains the medallions over the doorway, showing snakes entwined round a staff. This is doubtless the caduceus of Mercury, who was considered the protector of merchants and commercial buildings (*cf* Sir John Soane's serpent motif at the Bank of England). On the eastern side, all the buildings from Croftway to Platt's Lane were taken over (and recently abandoned) by (Queen Mary and) Westfield College of London University and called the Hampstead Campus. **No. 316** is labelled 'Department of French' and **No. 318** 'Department of German'. **No. 318A** is a converted coach house and **No. 322** has dragonets on its gables and dragonheads on its porch. There are more 1930s small-scale houses between Platt's Lane and Briardale Gardens. Here is the borough boundary, which then cuts across the top of Hendon Way and embraces three residential roads on the borders of Cricklewood.

BURGESS HILL takes its name from a prosperous Lancashireman, Henry Weech Burgess, who laid out an estate here in 1837: he called it Temple Park, as the fields he built over were known as Great and Little Temple Wood. (These reminders of the Knights Templar's local land ownership are commemorated by nearby Templewood Avenue.) The Tithe Map of 1839 shows two houses on the property and by 1873 one of these had been occupied by the Anglo-French College of Joseph Haysman (see above). A drive linked the College with Fortune Green Road. Another approach from Finchley Road followed the line of the present Burgess Hill. This road is shown on an 1862 map as Burgess Park Gardens and did not get its present name until it was rebuilt in 1903. The earliest houses here had rural names of a medieval flavour such as Meadside, Highclere and Fairholme. The present residences, except **Burnet House**, are all decidedly twentieth century. Much rebuilding followed the last war, when two flying bombs fell in this area. The adjoining **ARDWICK ROAD** commemorates not only Henry Burgess's home town in Lancashire but his son, Major Ardwick Burgess, who developed this property. The upper part of the road is seen on an 1862 map and was known as Ardwick Terrace until 1903, when the present name was approved.

RANULF ROAD was originally called Olive Road and followed the line of an old path connecting Platt's Lane and Cowhouse Farm in Hendon. Half the road is still in Hendon (the borough boundary comes just after Burgess Hill) but the name belongs entirely to Hampstead. Ranulf Peverel is featured in the Domesday Book's survey of Hampstead as the man who held one hide (about 120 acres) then worth five shillings. Barratt presumes that this was the same Peverel who was the Conqueror's favourite and who married William's discarded mistress, Ingelrica. His name-son, whom William had fathered, was supposed to become the *Peveril of the Peak* of Scott's historical romance. Among Ranulf Road's current residents is the writer and broadcaster Alan Coren, but, as his writings have defiantly declared, he is definitely at the Cricklewood end of the road. The views from this outpost of Hampstead are breathtaking and Cricklewood has never looked better.

ROUND FORTUNE GREEN

The origins of **FORTUNE GREEN ROAD** and of the Green itself are lost in medieval mists. The road follows an old track called Green Lane and is not named on maps until 1862, when it is shown as Fortune Green Lane. Its present title was approved in 1896. The name of Fortune Green is first recorded in 1646 and first seen on Rocque's map of 1746. Its derivation is uncertain. *The Place-Names of Middlesex* suggests that Fortune comes from 'foran-tune' meaning 'in front of the tun'. Was there perhaps a wine bar at this ancient crossroads? This was where the old Blind Lane (now disappeared) met the route from West End to Cow House Farm in Hendon. This latter path, though thrown somewhat off course by the Cemetery it bisects, still links up with Farm Avenue in Hendon. To the west of the path, a line of poplars is thought to mark the route of Blind Lane, which then crossed what is now Minster Road and made a right-angle turn to come out in Mill Lane.

Originally of about four acres, **Fortune Green** was a patch of manorial waste, where local residents had the right to graze animals, dig turf and play sports. A short history of the Green, on a council **noticeboard**, notes regular cricket matches, including married *v* singles, boxing, rounders and trapball. The Green dwindled considerably in the last century when the Lord of the Manor granted enclosure rights for about a third of the area. Nine cottages were built here from 1820, housing labourers and laundresses, who were allowed to keep drying poles on the Green for fourpence a year. In 1875, more of the open space was lost to the new Hampstead Cemetery and in the 1880s the whole area was threatened with redevelopment. The local population formed a Fortune Green Protection Society in 1891 and held protest meetings on the Green, attended by hundreds of residents. Particular objection was made against a gypsy encampment on the Green, and in December 1893, the Fortune Green Preservation Society called a meeting to fight this 'interference with public rights' and to evict the squatters. The meeting would be supported, the Society announced, by members of the Football and Athletic Club and their motto was *Fortuna Favet Fortibus*. The gypsies offered no resistance when the crowd marched up to their caravan and cut the chain which fastened it to a tree. They even folded their tent and silently stole away. But the Green still remained largely in the hands of the Lord of the Manor and £8,000 had to be raised to buy it for the public. An appeal was made to the Vestry, pointing out the shortage of open spaces in the West End area and that 'a visit to Hampstead Heath...in consequence of distance and steep gradients of the roads, demands more time and

35. Eviction of gypsies from Fortune Green, from the *Daily Graphic*, 1893.

physical exertion than a large number of persons can conveniently give'. The Vestry acknowledged this energy crisis and, with LCC help, provided most of the purchase price: however, £1,647 was collected by public subscription, over half of which came, as usual, from Sir Henry Harben. So the Green went public in 1897. (The story of *The Fight for Fortune Green* is told in *Camden History Review* No. 10.) After World War I, a number of captured German guns were displayed on the Green but these were removed and melted down in World War II. The Green has recently been enlarged after local preservationists claimed back an unused strip of the Cemetery. This land, now owned by the council, would have covered 900 graves or six years of interments but, as the Works Committee Councillor said: 'Six years' use as a burial space does not compare with an infinity of time as a playspace.' Today the Green offers a fenced-off **Play Centre** for children and every July joins in the local Jester Festival.

At the northern end of Fortune Green Road are the twenty-five acres of **Hampstead Cemetery**. Twenty of these acres were pastureland bought by the Burial Board in 1875 for £7,000. The small addition bought in 1901 from the Burgess Park estate was much dearer, costing £15,000. The Lodge and Chapel, which are now Listed Buildings, were built by Charles Bell in 1875/6 and the two-thirds of the ground reserved for Church of England burials was consecrated by the Bishop of London the following year. Many artistic people of note were among the early arrivals here, including the artists, Kate Greenaway (of Frognal) and Edwin Long (of Fitzjohns Avenue), and the architect Banister Fletcher senior (of Woodchurch Road). Other Hampstead celebrities here are George Jealous, proprietor and editor of the *Ham and High*, and two industrialists who lived at the foot of Fitzjohns Avenue, Frank Debenham (but no Freebody) and Samuel Palmer (but no Huntley). The pioneer of antiseptic surgery, Lord Lister, was buried here in 1912, declining an interment in Westminster Abbey because he preferred to lie here, next to his wife, Agnes. Other pioneers include the Short Brothers, famous for their aircraft, and Florence Upton, creator of the golliwog. Grand Duke Michael of Russia (1861–1929), cousin of Nicholas II, is buried here with his wife, Sophie: their morganatic marriage forced his exile from Russia and for some years he lived at Kenwood House. Another eminence from overseas is Andrew Fisher (1862–1928), three times Prime Minister of Australia. The stage is represented by actor Fred Terry, Henry Arthur Jones, playwright, Marie Lloyd, music-hall queen, and by the bizarre Bianchi monument, erected in the 1930s by an Italian restaurateur to his opera-singer wife. Other curiosities are an organ-shaped tomb, a monument inscribed entirely in shorthand and a colonnaded tomb for Pasha James Wilson, who served as an engineer with the Egyptian Government. Recent burials include actors Clive Brook and Gladys Cooper, horn virtuoso Dennis Brain and novelists John Braine, Gilbert and Pamela Frankau and Nigel Balchin, whose stone records only the title of one of his novels: 'Lord, I Was Afraid'. One of the handsomest monuments in the cemetery is on the grave of Sir William Goscombe John (1860–1952) – a bronze figure sculpted by him in memory of his wife, Martha, who was buried here in 1923.

Continuing down the west side of Fortune Green Road, a **garage** and **The Prince of Wales** are on that part of Fortune Green lost to the public in the nineteenth century. (The last two cottages were suddenly demolished in 1989.) The pub, originally a beer parlour, was rebuilt in 1965 in weatherboarded cottage style and totally refurbished in 1985/6. At the southern tip of the Green is a **fountain** erected by the Cattle Trough Association, a proper reminder that this was for centuries a popular thoroughfare for the cattle of North London.

Past the fish and chip **restaurant** ('probably the best in London' said *The Times*), the **Police Station** was built in 1972 to the designs of J. Innes Elliot, chief architect to New Scotland Yard. It took over business from the station at 90 West End Lane, and now houses one of London's few Mounted Police Divisions. The premises are on the site of Berridge House, opened in 1908 as part of the National Society's Training College for Teachers of Domestic Subjects. The original Berridge House was demolished in 1966, when the college moved to Tottenham but its name was preserved until recently on a building in Hillfield Road (*q.v.*).

Returning up the east side of Fortune Green Road (note Victorian **postbox** at the corner with Lyncroft Gardens), **Holly Mansions** is all that remains of a series of houses with arboreal names. Laurel, Beech, Oak and Willow Mansions have now disappeared and **Walter Northcott House** flourishes instead. The plaque on these flats records that Alderman Northcott was a local councillor from 1909 for 53 years. The old houses were destroyed by bombing in the last war, which included a flying-bomb in 1944. **Nos. 38–44** have a nice burst of terracotta sunflowers; No. 38 was for many years Lymington House School. Robert Mair cobbled at **No. 86** from the 1920s to the 1960s and his sign can still be seen on the wall above – 'Boot Repairs, Quality Work'. **No. 118**, a newsagents since 1890, has been run by the Loder family for over half a century. Next door, **Weech Hall** was built in the late 1930s on the site of All Souls

Unitarian Church. Westmount is the name of the new **No. 126**, sheltered housing for the elderly, opened in 1976 by Elizabeth Corob. The ornate **No. 128** is the one survivor of a pair of late nineteenth century buildings, once owned by undertakers and designed to catch the eye of visitors to the Cemetery opposite. Thanks to its Graeco-Egyptian stucco pastiche, it is included in the DoE's List of Buildings 'for curiosity value'.

To the east of Fortune Green Road, a number of small residential streets grew up mostly in the 1880s. Starting from the north, **WEECH ROAD** was in 1880 one of the first to be built. The name derives from Henry Weech Burgess of nearby Burgess Hill (*q.v.*). As with other roads in the area, the residents here from the beginning included a large proportion of single people and many more women than men, probably because most households had one or two servants. In fact, early this century half the employed female population of Hampstead was in some sort of domestic service. **No. 16** is one of several houses here with original stained glass doors.

INGHAM ROAD and **BURRARD ROAD** were built in 1885 by the National Standard Land Mortgage and Investment Company Limited. Edward Ingham was the Manager and Burrard may have been the name of another official. Ingham Road was first called Oakland Crescent while Burrard Road took over College Villas and College Terrace, named after the nearby Hackney (now Parsifal) College. To start with, the latter street gave homes to many builders, plasterers and plumbers but early this century its image improved: it was then that the dressmakers at **No. 38**, the Misses Godden and Evans, appeared in the Directory as Mesdames Godden and Evans. Ingham Road was much enhanced by the planting in 1983 of cherry, alder, rowan and other decorative trees. The houses are nearly all of the same design with much flora and foliage. **PARSIFAL ROAD** is altogether more impressive: its grand name was approved in 1883, the year after Wagner's opera burst upon London. **No. 1** was the vicarage of Emmanuel Church from 1894 to 1968. An unusual stained glass window to the side of the house shows a female figure thought to represent Poetry. The site of **No. 3** has been boarded up for several years and at one time had a pond, which was popular with ducks, newts and frogs. Did they belatedly inspire the sculptor living in the 1970s at **No. 5**, Phillip King, one of whose exhibits at the 1991 RA summer show was *The Frog Jumps*? **Nos. 7–9**, with their terracotta faces, are among many well-ornamented houses in the road.

LYNCROFT GARDENS was not built until 1895 and, though the name appears to be a fanciful one, it may be connected with the country seat, Lyncroft, near Lichfield. The houses are good and solid with some decorative tiles in the porches on the west side. The road follows the line of a footpath across the grounds of what was Woodbine Cottage, the home from 1854 to 1872 of the famous Eley brothers, makers of gun cartridges. Their father had been 'blown to atoms' at his factory in Old Bond Street and their mother died from cholera soon after her arrival at the cottage. There was no cholera in West End but Mrs Eley so liked the water from a pump in Broad Street that she had a bottle of it delivered every day: she was one of 600 who died from drinking the infected water. Around 1860 the gentry of Hampstead gladly came to shoot at the Eleys' butts, on the site of Parsifal Road, but local girls refused to work in their factory here for fear of being blown up. By 1885 Woodbine Cottage belonged to the society beauty, Mrs Laura Thistlethwayte. An Irish lady of humble origins, whose face was her fortune (see picture in Barratt), she came to West End as a wealthy widow. Here she received her famous friends, notably Mr and Mrs Gladstone (the Grand Old Man was said to be infatuated with her) and laid out her grounds with greenhouses, stables and a paddock full of deer. A notice on the fence facing Cannon Hill warned: 'Trespassers – Beware of Man-Traps and Spring Guns'. The row of lime trees outside the church on West End Green is all that is left of her property. **No. 43** Lyncroft Gardens, faintly labelled 'Polperro Mansions', was the home of Leopold Lowenstamm, whose etchings were frequently seen at the Royal Academy in the 1880s. Among current residents in the street is another frequent exhibitor at the Academy, Norman Blamey RA.

Emmanuel Church was built on one corner of the Woodbine Cottage estate, graduating to this eventual 800-seater from a small Mission Church in Mill Lane. Before that, the few souls of West End had been watched over variously by the Parish Church, by St Paul's in Avenue Road and by what became Holy Trinity in Finchley Road. The Mission Church was built at the corner of Aldred Road in 1875 and it thrived under the curateship of the Reverend Edmund Davys.'Recently returned from missionary work in China', says a church history, 'he asked his old friend Mr Sharpe (of Holy Trinity) if he knew of a small charge where he could quietly end his days. Mr Sharpe's reply was' "Come to West End…".' Mr Davys who was, in fact, only fifty-nine, became the first vicar of Emmanuel when it achieved its independence in 1884 under the New Parishes Act. It is now the biggest parish in Hampstead. The chancel and first four bays of the present church were erected in 1898 and the rest was added in 1903. In this year the Mission Church was demolished and proceeds from the sale helped to build the new Parish Hall in Broomsleigh Street. The architects for both church and hall were Whitfield and Thomas. The church has a Salisbury Chapel, commemorating the artist Frank Salisbury, who painted the altar picture in memory of his wife and designed the two stained glass windows. Salisbury lived for many years at Sarum Chase in West Heath Road. One of the first organists at Emmanuel was the composer, Martin Shaw (see also *The Streets of Belsize*). In his memoirs he recalled that he used to affect a cloak, sandals and long hair at this period, and commented: 'The amazing thing is that any respectable body of people could have swallowed me so long.' Emmanuel must be one of the first churches to have a built-on **vicarage**. This addition was designed by a recent vicar, the Rev. Jack Dover Wellman, once a naval architect and designer of a mini-submarine. (A full history of the church has been written by Jennifer Tucker.)

CANNON HILL was built by Charles Cannon, a prosperous dye merchant, who became official dyer to Queen Victoria. Mr Cannon, who lived at nearby Kidderpore Hall (see *The Streets of Hampstead*), widened an old footpath running alongside a stream (sometimes known as Cannon's Stream), which rose in Branch Hill, filled the pond at West End Green, and contributed to the river Westbourne. The road is shown and named on Stanford's 1862 map but it was not built up until 1900, when **Marlborough Mansions** were erected and completely filled it on both sides. Residents have included the novelist, Nigel Balchin, who died here in 1970; the conductor, Sir Adrian Boult, and the artist Sir William Coldstream, who lived as a boy in Garlinge Road (*q.v.*), near Kilburn High Road. Did his family know that the name Kilburn may derive from 'kyle-bourne' meaning 'cold stream'?

EAST OF WEST END LANE

In 1897 four roads were laid out between West End Lane and Finchley Road, all named after pretty towns or villages in South and West England. In the absence of other evidence, it must be assumed that the place-names had sentimental attractions for the exploiters of the land. **HONEYBOURNE ROAD** recalls the Worcestershire villages of Church and Cow Honeybourne but consists almost entirely of large blocks of flats named **Harvard** and **Yale Courts**, presumably after the two premier American universities. This road cuts right across the estate of West End Hall and still has its original Edwardian **postbox**.

The adjoining estate of Treherne House was invaded by **FAWLEY ROAD**, a name that recalls a number of villages, notably in Herefordshire and Hampshire. This street was a late developer, with only a few houses in its early years, but from the start it was favoured by professional men, especially doctors, and even one artist. The prolific composer, Sir Henry Walford Davies, lived at **No. 21** between 1901–11. He had been organist at Christ Church, Hampstead, in the 1890s and was befriended by the music-loving Matheson family, who lived in nearby Cannon Place. He later joined their household and moved with them to Acton and Golders Green. Soon after his arrival in Fawley Road he conducted the first performance of his cantata,

Everyman, before a select audience in the front hall of his home.

CREDITON HILL (until 1907 Crediton Road) presumably took its name from the town in Devonshire. The first resident here was Captain Cuthbert Keeson, whose house was originally known as **No. 1** but by 1904 was called St Cuthbert's. It is not known who effected the canonisation. Between 1929 and 1937 this was the home of York House School. Crediton Hill has always had a respectable and leisurely air and its architectural styles are a cut above its neighbours'. Its proximity to the cricket and tennis clubs must surely have helped. **No. 20** has a grand pillared porch. The builder of **No. 30** was Robert Vernon Hart of Briardale Gardens, where he built many similar houses. In 1906, the cost of the original No. 30 was £1,100, a considerable sum at the time. Eric Thompson (1929–82), the creator of the *Magic Roundabout* (and father of actresses Emma and Sophie) lived at **No. 31** from 1970 until his death.

LYMINGTON ROAD may have had the same originator as Fawley Road, as Lymington is nine miles west of Fawley in Hampshire. The road follows the old path from Finchley Road to the original pavilion of the **Hampstead Cricket Club**. This club migrated here in 1877 after using grounds in the Elsworthy Road area and later one near Abbey Road.

When the latter was wanted for building development, the Lord of the Manor, Sir Spencer Maryon Wilson, offered this alternative site on a very favourable lease. The Club soon became popular, helped perhaps by the cask of beer available free to members, while 'temperance drinks' cost 4d a bottle. The grounds were also alive with the sound of hockey and tennis but the hockey section got out of hand and in 1893 it was closed down. By 1924 the surrounding area was fully built up and the landlord warned the Club that they must buy or quit. £25,000 was quickly raised in a popular appeal, finally fathered by the local celebrity, Sir Gerald du Maurier. £5,000 came from The Hall School, in exchange for fifteen years' use of the grounds, and £3,000 was contributed by Mrs Wharrie, daughter of Sir Henry Harben. During the last war, the RAF Balloon Section took over part of the grounds and the pavilion. But the Club's finest hour was surely in August 1887, when they scored a total of 813 runs, including A.E. Stoddart's innings of 485, against a team appropriately called The Stoics.

Much of the south side of this road is now occupied by Camden Council's **Lymington Road Estate** completed in 1979. The names of the roads offer varieties of porcelain, from Crown Close, through Doulton, Minton, Worcester, Beswick, Spode and Wedgwood to Dresden Close. No reason for this has been recorded. The Edwardian **pillar-box** nearby seems out of period. The remaining houses in the street are mostly substantial originals, some of which have curious faces on their canopy supports. Among these is **No. 28**, the home of Edmund Clerihew Bentley (1875–1956), when he was a leader-writer for the *Daily Telegraph* in the 1920s. He was also author of the famous *Trent's Last Case* (1913), 'the milestone in the transformation of the de-tective novel from the romantic to the realistic' (Chambers), and of those rhyming tags called clerihews. **Nos. 22–24** have notable plaster figures up top. The old **No. 21** was the home of Tomás Harris (1908–64) described in the *DNB* as artist, art dealer and intelligence officer: his *DNB* entry was written by Anthony Blunt, who said of Harris: 'His greatest achievement was as one of the principal organisers of Operation Garbo, the most successful double-cross operation of the last war': this Operation misled the Germans about the Allied invasion plans in 1944.

ALVANLEY GARDENS was the last road in this area to be developed. The layout is spacious and the houses are quite large. The street name was approved in 1914 and derives from the distinguished lawyer, Richard Pepper Arden, Lord Alvanley (1745–1804), who lived at Frognal Hall and who derived his title from his family's estate in Cheshire. Sir Archibald Gray (1880–1967), a distinguished dermatologist, lived at **No. 7** up to his death. **No. 6** was for many years, up to the late 1980s, the home of the Cohen family, a quartet of distinguished musicians, including Raymond (violin) and Robert (cello). The **Cumberland Lawn Tennis Club** arrived here in 1903, before the road was built. The club had begun in 1880, when ten men played regularly on a court in Regent's Park and christened their club after nearby Cumberland Terrace. As with its neighbouring cricketers, the club first leased the ground from the Lord of the Manor and then bought it from him in the 1920s. The clubhouse built at this time has been progressively enlarged, and similarly the Open Tournament, inaugurated in 1927, has now grown to an important Spring event in the annual Wimbledon warm-up.

INDEX

Streets included in the survey and the main entry for them are indicated in bold type. Page numbers with asterisks indicate illustrations.

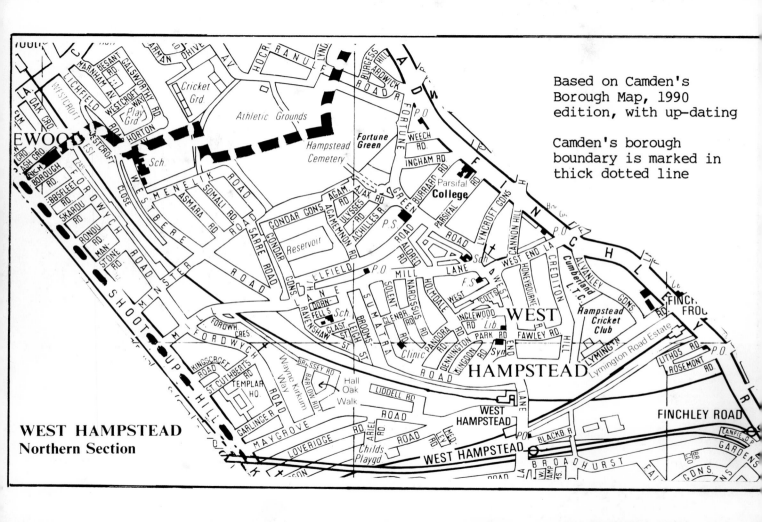

Based on Camden's
Borough Map, 1990
edition, with up-dating

Camden's borough
boundary is marked in
thick dotted line

WEST HAMPSTEAD
Northern Section